ECCE ROMANI

A Latin Reading Course
Prepared by The Scottish Classics Group

3
Home and School

Second Edition

Oliver & Boyd

Illustrated by Trevor Parkin
Cover illustration by Peter Dennis

Oliver & Boyd
Robert Stevenson House
1–3 Baxter's Place
Leith Walk
Edinburgh EH1 3BB

A Division of Longman Group Limited

First published 1972
Second edition 1983
Second impression 1985

ISBN 0 05 003467 7

Printed in Hong Kong by
Commonwealth Printing Press Ltd

Contents

28
Going Shopping

mane erat. Aurelia in cubiculo sedebat. crines eius curabant duae ancillae, quarum altera speculum tenebat, altera crines pectebat. Phrygia, quae crines neglegenter pectebat, dominam vexabat; Syra, quod manus tremebat, speculum non bene tenebat. Aurelia igitur, neglegentia earum vexata, subito "quam neglegentes estis!" clamavit. "abite! abite! vocate Corneliam! eam mecum in urbem ducere volo."

statim exierunt ancillae.

mox in cubiculum iniit Cornelia. "cur me vocavisti, mater?"

cui Aurelia "pater tuus amicos quosdam, in quibus sunt senatores praeclari, ad cenam hodie invitavit. porcum servi iam emerunt, sed ego in animo habeo ipsa in urbem ire ad mercatorem quendam cuius taberna non procul abest, nam glires optimos ille vendere solet. si tu vis mecum ire, me in atrio exspecta! interea servos iubebo sellas ad ianuam ferre."

Cornelia summa celeritate se paravit. brevi tempore mater et filia a servis per urbem ferebantur. in viis erat ingens multitudo hominum. concursabant enim servi, milites, viri, pueri, mulieres. onera ingentia a servis portabantur, nam interdiu nihil intra urbem vehiculo portatur.

omnia quae videt Cornelia eam delectant. nunc conspicit poetam versus recitantem, nunc mendicos pecuniam petentes, nunc lecticam elegantissimam quae ab octo servis portatur. in ea recumbit homo obesus qui librum legit.

subito Cornelia duos servos per viam festinantes conspicit, quorum alter porcum parvulum portat. eo ipso tempore e manibus effugit porcus. "cavete!" exclamant adstantes, sed frustra. homo quidam, qui per viam celeriter currit, porcum vitare non potest. ad terram cadit. paulisper in luto iacet gemens. deinde ira commotus servum petit. est rixa.

finem rixae non vidit Cornelia quod servi iam sellas in aliam viam tulerant. tandem advenerunt ad eam tabernam quam petebant. de sellis descenderunt. tum Aurelia "vidistine" inquit "illam lecticam in qua recumbebat homo obesus? unus ex libertis Caesaris ipsius … sed quid accidit? fumum video et flammas."

crines, crinium (*m.pl*), hair
alter, altera, alterum, the one, the other (of two)
speculum, -i (*n*), mirror
neglegenter, carelessly
vexatus, -a, -um, annoyed
mecum, with me
in quibus, among whom
porcus, -i (*m*), pig
cuius, whose
glis, gliris (*m*), dormouse
sella, -ae (*f*), sedan chair
summa celeritate, with the greatest speed, as fast as possible
a servis ferebantur, were being carried by slaves

concurso (1), to run to and fro, run about
portatur, is (being) carried
delecto (1), to delight
mendicus, -i (*m*), beggar
elegantissimus, -a, -um, most elegant
adstantes, adstantium (*m.pl*), bystanders
rixa, -ae (*f*), quarrel
finis, finis (*m*), end
libertus, -i (*m*), freedman
ipsius, genitive sing. of **ipse, ipsa, ipsum**
fumus, -i (*m*), smoke

pecto, pectere (3), **pexi, pexum,** to comb
vendo, vendere (3), **vendidi, venditum,** to sell
recumbo, recumbere (3), **recubui,** to recline

VERBS: the Vivid or Historic Present

In Story 28, the verbs in the paragraphs beginning "omnia quae videt Cornelia" and "subito Cornelia duos servos" are in the present tense although they describe past events. The effect of this is to make the reader feel that he personally is sharing in Cornelia's experience.

The use of the present tense adds vividness (as in this story) and, where the story requires it, speed and excitement. Written English normally uses a past tense to describe such actions.

Notice that in the final paragraph ("finem rixae non vidit..."), where the narrative resumes, the writer returns to the past tense.

The Relative Pronoun

You have now met all the forms of the relative pronoun:

	Singular			Meanings
	Masc.	Fem.	Neut.	
Nom.	qui	quae	quod	who, which
Acc.	quem	quam	quod	whom, which
Gen.	cuius	cuius	cuius	whose, of whom, of which
Dat.	cui	cui	cui	to whom (which), for whom (which)
Abl.	quo	qua	quo	(see examples below)

	Plural			Meanings
	Masc.	Fem.	Neut.	
Nom.	qui	quae	quae	who, which
Acc.	quos	quas	quae	whom, which
Gen.	quorum	quarum	quorum	whose, of whom, of which
Dat.	quibus	quibus	quibus	to whom (which), for whom (which)
Abl.	quibus	quibus	quibus	(see examples below)

The following sentences show the meanings of the ablative case:

> servi, **a quibus** lectica ferebatur, ingentes erant.
> *The slaves **by whom** the litter was being carried were huge.*

> puellae, **a quibus** librum emeram, amicae meae erant.
> *The girls **from whom** I had bought the book were my friends.*

> celavit gladium **quo** hominem necaverat.
> *He hid the sword **with which** he had killed the fellow.*

> amici **quibuscum** iter faciebam me servaverunt.
> *The friends **with whom** I was travelling saved me.*

Note: The word to which the relative pronoun refers is called the *antecedent* (i.e. the word which "goes before"). The relative pronoun agrees with its antecedent in *number* and *gender*; its *case* depends on its use in its own clause. Observe the examples above.

Exercise 28a

Translate:

1 servi, qui cistas portabant, huc illuc concursabant. cistae, quas servi portabant, plenae erant vestium.
2 ancillae, quae Aureliae crines curabant, dominam timebant. Aurelia, quae multis rebus sollicita erat, ancillas neglegentes abire iussit.
3 servus, a quo onus portabatur, gemebat. onus enim, quod portabat, ingens erat.
4 omnia aedificia, quae pueri videbant, iam sunt ruinae. illae ruinae, quas nos hodie videmus, pulchrae adhuc sunt.
5 porci, quos servi portabant, grunniebant. adstantes, qui eos audiebant, erant perterriti.

pulcher, pulchra, pulchrum, beautiful

Exercise 28b

Give the Latin for the relative pronoun (in brackets) and then translate the sentence:

1 homo, (who) per viam currebat, ad terram cecidit.
2 ancilla, (who) crines neglegenter pectebat, Aureliam vexabat.
3 homo obesus, (whom) servi portabant, librum legebat.
4 Aurelia, (whom) ancillae vexabant, speculum eripuit.
5 duo servi, (whom) Cornelia conspexit, per viam festinabant.
6 brevi tempore mater et filia sellas, (which) servi tulerant, ascenderunt.
7 puella, (to whom) librum dedi, erat Cornelia.
8 servus, (whose) dominus erat iratus, statim aufugit.

Exercise 28c

Translate:

1 aurigae, quorum equi sunt celerrimi, non semper victoriam habent.
2 Aurelia, cui mercator glires vendidit, pecuniam magnam secum ferebat.
3 hi amici, quibuscum ad amphitheatrum cras ibimus, feriati erunt.
4 cives, quorum clamores audivimus, aurigas spectabant.
5 hanc urbem, in qua habitamus, valde amamus.

6 milites, quibus Caesar signum dedit, spectatores e Circo removerunt.
7 homo obesus, cuius lectica erat elegantissima, librum legebat.
8 cubiculum, in quo ancillae dominae crines curabant, non erat magnum.
9 Aurelia et Cornelia, quarum stolae erant elegantissimae, ipsae pulchrae erant.
10 nemo capere poterat porcum, qui e manibus servi effugerat.

capio, capere (3), **cepi, captum,** to take, capture

Town House and Tenement

A wealthy Roman like Cornelius would normally possess, in addition to his town house (**domus**), at least one country house (**villa rustica**). Cicero had several, where he could get away from the city din and summer heat, but even a **domus** provided considerable privacy and seclusion.

Plan of a domus

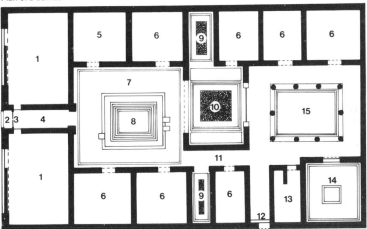

1 **tabernae** (shops)
2 **vestibulum** (entrance outside **ianua**)
3 **ianua** (double door)
4 **fauces** (entrance passage)
5 **cella** (room for doorkeeper)
6 **cubicula** (bedrooms)
7 **atrium** (hall)
8 **compluvium/impluvium** (roof opening and tank)
9 **ala** (alcove)
10 **tablinum** (study)
11 **andron** (passage)
12 **posticum** (servants' entrance)
13 **culina** (kitchen)
14 **triclinium** (dining room)
15 **peristylium** (garden)

It was self-contained and usually built on one level with few, if any, windows on its outside walls. It faced inwards and most of its light came from the opening in the roof of the main hall

9

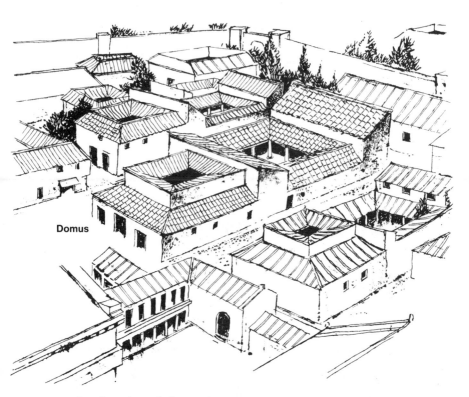

Domus

(**atrium**) and from the open colonnaded garden (**peristylium**). Grouped around these open areas were the purpose-
built rooms of the house—bedrooms (**cubicula**), study
(**tablinum**), kitchen area (**culina**), dining room (**triclinium**), etc. Decoration and furniture in the **domus** was as
splendid as its owner's pocket allowed, and in some cases a
second storey was added. The domus-style house can be
identified in towns throughout the Roman world.

Where building space was at a premium, as in a city like
Rome or a commercial town like Ostia, houses tended to grow
upwards to accommodate the majority of the inhabitants.
These tenement-type houses were called **insulae**. Sometimes
they stood four or five storeys high and restrictions were
introduced as early as the time of the Emperor Augustus to
prevent their height exceeding 20 metres (70 feet).

Brick and concrete were commonly used in their construction,
and they often had large windows and doorways enhancing
their external appearance. The same rooms in the building
tended to serve various functions, and there was a uniformity

about the plan of each flat in the building. Wooden shutters or canvas screens kept out the elements. Running water was rarely available above ground level, so heating and cooking often proved a hazard. Ground floor accommodation in the **insulae** was usually the most desirable.

While **insulae** could be very attractive and were often built around large central courts, some were less presentable. Often single rooms were let and conditions were cramped. Excessive reliance on wood and plaster construction led to the risk of fire or collapse, and after the fire of AD 64 the Emperor Nero introduced tighter control of building materials in the **insulae**.

Life could also be unpleasantly noisy, since the ground floor often housed shops of various descriptions. On the ground floor of the **insula** in which Seneca, a Roman writer, had his flat there was a public bath, and he describes some of the noises which disturbed him: the great splash made by the swimmer who likes to dive in as noisily as he can; the slapping sounds as people are being rubbed down; the noises of the man who likes to hear his own voice in the bath; the shouts of the pastrycook and the sausage-maker trying to sell their wares. Martial tells us of a schoolmaster who began shouting at his pupils in the early morning and kept his neighbours from sleeping.

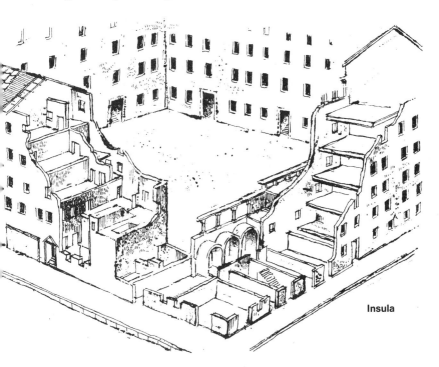

Insula

29
Fire!

conspexerat Aurelia magnam insulam ex qua emittebatur magna vis fumi ac flammarum. Cornelia iam ad id aedificium summa celeritate currebat cum Aurelia ei clamavit "cave, Cornelia! ei incendio appropinquare est periculosum."

mox fumus omnia obscurabat. Cornelia aedificium ipsum vix videre poterat. multi homines huc illuc concursabant. ab incolis omnia simul aguntur; infantes ex aedificio a matribus efferuntur; infirmi ex ianuis trahuntur; bona ex fenestris eiciuntur; in via ponuntur cistae, lecti, ornamenta.

Cornelia spectaculum tam miserabile numquam antea viderat. lacrimabant mulieres et liberos parvos tenebant; lacrimabant liberi qui parentes suos quaerebant; clamabant parentes qui liberos suos petebant.

via erat plena eorum qui ad spectaculum venerant. alii ex adstantibus aquam portabant; alii in insulam intrabant et auxilium ad incolas miseros ferebant. multi tamen nihil faciebant. "nos certe nihil facere possumus" inquiunt. "in hac urbe solent esse incendia quae exstinguere non possumus. neque hoc aedificium neque hos incolas servare possumus. ecce! in tertio tabulato huius insulae est mater cum duobus liberis. hi miseri flammis paene opprimuntur. si incolae se servare non possunt, quid nos facere possumus?"

subito exclamavit unus ex adstantibus "cavete, omnes! nisi statim aufugietis, vos omnes opprimemini aut lapidibus aut flammis."

tum Cornelia "eheu, mater!" inquit "ego valde commoveor cum hos tam miseros liberos video. quis ad eos auxilium feret? quomodo effugient? quid eis accidet?"

cui respondit Aurelia "id nescio. sine dubio iam mortui sunt. sed cur tu ita commoveris? nos nihil hic facere possumus. nisi statim fugiemus, nos ipsae vix servabimur. satis tamen hodie vidisti. age! ad forum ibimus ac glires ememus."

illo ipso tempore muri insulae magno fragore ceciderunt. nihil manebat nisi lapides ac fumus.

insula, -ae (*f*), tenement

ac, and

incendium, -i (*n*), fire

vix, scarcely, with difficulty, only just

incola, -ae (*m*), tenant

omnia aguntur, everything is being done

infirmus, -a, -um, frail

fenestra, -ae (*f*), window

ornamenta, -orum (*n.pl*), furnishings

tam, so

parvus, -a, -um, small

solent esse incendia, there are regular outbreaks of fire

in tertio tabulato, on the third floor

paene, almost

opprimuntur, (they) are being overwhelmed

opprimemini, you will be overwhelmed

aut ... aut ..., either ... or ...

commoveor, I am upset

sine dubio, without doubt

commoveris, you are upset

servabimur, we shall be saved

eicio, eicere (3), **eieci, eiectum,** to throw out

quaero, quaerere (3), **quaesivi, quaesitum,** to seek, look for

opprimo, opprimere (3), **oppressi, oppressum,** to overwhelm

commoveo, commovere (2), **commovi, commotum,** to move

VERBS: Active and Passive

Compare the following sentences:

incolae omnia **agunt**.
The tenants are doing everything.

ab incolis omnia **aguntur**.
Everything is being done by the tenants.

matres infantes **efferunt**.
The mothers carry out the babies.

infantes a matribus **efferuntur**.
The babies are carried out by the mothers.

servi onera **portabant**.
Slaves were carrying the loads.

onera a servis **portabantur**.
The loads were being carried by slaves.

flammae vos **oppriment**.
The flames will overwhelm you.

vos flammis **opprimemini**.
You will be overwhelmed by the flames.

The verbs in the left-hand column are *active voice*; in the right-hand column the verbs are *passive voice*.

The following table gives the forms and meanings of the present indicative passive of **mitto**:

	Singular		Plural
1	mitto**r**, I am (being) sent	1	mitti**mur**, we are (being) sent
2	mitte**ris**, you are (being) sent	2	mitti**mini**, you are (being) sent
3	mitti**tur**, he, she, it is (being) sent	3	mittu**ntur**, they are (being) sent

Present Indicative Passive

		Group 1	Group 2	Group 3	Group 4
	1	porto**r**	moveo**r**	mitto**r**	audio**r**
S	2	porta**ris**	move**ris**	mittĕ**ris**	audi**ris**
	3	porta**tur**	move**tur**	mitti**tur**	audi**tur**
	1	porta**mur**	move**mur**	mitti**mur**	audi**mur**
P	2	porta**mini**	move**mini**	mitti**mini**	audi**mini**
	3	porta**ntur**	move**ntur**	mittu**ntur**	audiu**ntur**

Future Indicative Passive

	1	porta**bor**	move**bor**	mitt**ar**	audi**ar**
S	2	porta**beris**	move**beris**	mittĕ**ris**	audi**eris**
	3	porta**bitur**	move**bitur**	mitt**etur**	audi**etur**
	1	porta**bimur**	move**bimur**	mitt**emur**	audi**emur**
P	2	porta**bimini**	move**bimini**	mitt**emini**	audi**emini**
	3	porta**buntur**	move**buntur**	mitt**entur**	audi**entur**

Imperfect Indicative Passive

		Group 1	Group 2	Group 3	Group 4
	1	porta**bar**	move**bar**	mitte**bar**	audie**bar**
S	2	porta**baris**	move**baris**	mitte**baris**	audie**baris**
	3	porta**batur**	move**batur**	mitte**batur**	audie**batur**
	1	porta**bamur**	move**bamur**	mitte**bamur**	audie**bamur**
P	2	porta**bamini**	move**bamini**	mitte**bamini**	audie**bamini**
	3	porta**bantur**	move**bantur**	mitte**bantur**	audie**bantur**

Exercise 29a

Translate:

1 adstantes auxilium ferebant; auxilium ab adstantibus ferebatur.
2 mulieres liberos tenebant; liberi a mulieribus tenebantur.
3 amici incolas servabunt; incolae ab amicis servabuntur.
4 flammae hos miseros opprimunt; hi miseri flammis opprimentur.
5 liberi parentes quaerunt; parentes a liberis quaeruntur.
6 incolae ornamenta e fenestris eiciebant; ornamenta e fenestris ab
  incolis eiciebantur.

Exercise 29b

Translate:

1 sella portatur; sella portabatur; sella portabitur.
2 Cornelia commovetur; Cornelia commovebitur; Cornelia
  commovebatur.
3 nihil agebatur; nihil agetur; nihil agitur.
4 strepitus auditur; strepitus audietur; strepitus audiebatur.
5 adstantes removebuntur; portae claudentur; liberi excitantur;
  epistolae scribuntur; servi custodiebantur.

Exercise 29c

Name the group to which the verb belongs, and then translate:

1 commoveris.   5 incendium procul videtur.
2 eicieris.   6 clamores audientur.
3 auxilium petetur.   7 spectatores e Circo removentur.
4 opprimemini.   8 vestes novae ab Aurelia hodie
                        gerentur.

Exercise 29d

Using story 29 as a guide, and making changes where necessary, translate into Latin:

1 The babies were being carried out of the building.
2 A mother with her two children was being overwhelmed by the
  flames.
3 Soon trunks were being placed in the street.
4 Take care, all of you! Soon you will be crushed by the stones.
5 Who will bring help to these children? What will happen to them?

Hazards of City Life

In cool Praeneste or Volsinii built among the wooded hills, who fears or ever has feared the collapse of a house? We live in a city largely propped up by slender poles; for this is how the inspector stops the houses falling down and, plastering over old cracks, he bids us sleep secure with disaster hanging over us. We should live where there are no fires, no alarms in the night. By the time the smoke has reached you who are still sleeping on the third floor, Ucalegon on the ground floor is already calling for water and removing his bits and pieces of furniture. For if there is an alarm on the ground floor, the last to burn will be the one protected from the rain only by the tiles where the gentle pigeons lay their eggs.

Juvenal, *Satires III.190*

Now take a look at the other, different dangers of the night. What a height to the high roofs from where a potsherd strikes your head whenever cracked or broken vessels fall from the windows! With what a weight they mark and score the pavement as they strike it! You could be considered lazy and lacking in foresight, if you go out to dine without first making your will. There are as many forms of death as there are open watchful windows as you pass by. Therefore you should wish and pray, poor thing, that they may be satisfied with emptying their slop-pails.

Juvenal, *Satires III.268*

The inconsiderate shopkeeper had robbed us of our whole city by not keeping his shop within its proper limits. You, Germanicus, have given orders for our narrow streets to grow; and what was once a path is now a road. No tavern door-post now is cluttered with flagons chained to it; a praetor is not forced to walk through the mud, nor is the barber allowed to wave his razor about dangerously among the thick-packed crowd; no longer does some dirty café block the whole street. The barber, café-owner, cook and butcher now keep within bounds. Now Rome is Rome; of late it was one big shop.

Martial, *Epigrams VII. 61*

Whether the disaster that followed was an accident or was deliberately started by the Emperor is not known, as the historians give both versions. However, it was worse and caused more damage than any other fire that has ever broken out in this city. It started in that part of the Circus nearest the Palatine and Caelian hills, among shops keeping inflammable goods; and the wind caused it to spread fiercely and rapidly along the whole length of the Circus. As the houses and temples here were not separated by solid walls and there was nothing to stop the blaze, it first spread furiously through the level parts, then rose up the hills, then down again to devastate the lower areas. It was too fast to be checked by any means whatsoever, the city being completely vulnerable because of the narrow, winding passages and haphazard streets characteristic of old Rome.

Tacitus, Annals XV. 38

But the parts of the city not taken up by Nero's Golden House were not, as happened after Rome was burned by the Gauls, built up in a haphazard, random fashion, but with regularly spaced streets and broad avenues; a limit was put upon the height of the buildings and there were open spaces with colonnades added to protect the fronts of the blocks of flats. Nero promised to pay the cost of these colonnades and to hand over the open spaces to the landlords, after they were cleared of rubble.

The buildings, up to a fixed height, were to be solidly built of stone from Gabii or Alba, material which is fireproof. No timber was to be used. Inspectors were appointed to ensure a more plentiful supply of water for public use; for individuals had been diverting it for their own private use. Water was to be made available at more points, and every open area was to contain fire-fighting appliances. Each building was to be enclosed by its own separate wall, instead of a common wall.

These regulations, introduced for practical reasons, brought beauty to the city. However, there were people who held that the old style was more healthy since the narrow streets and high buildings blotted out the heat of the sun more, whereas the open, unshaded spaces became far more oppressively hot.

Tacitus, Annals XV. 43

30
Pseudolus
Caught Out

quinta hora est. Marcus et Sextus per atrium ambulant, cum subito ex culina cachinnus maximus auditur. statim in culinam pueri intrant, ubi Syrum et alios servos vident.

Sextus "cur vos omnes ridetis?" inquit. "iocumne audivistis?"

cui Syrus "ioco optimo delectamur, domine. est in culina servus quidam cui nomen est Pseudolus. non servus sed mercator esse videtur. heri mane in urbem ad lanii tabernam descendit, nam carnem emere volebat. 'quanti' inquit Pseudolus 'est illa perna?' ubi pretium auditur, lanio respondet 'ego numquam dabo tantum pretium. praedo quidem mihi videris, non lanius. nemo nisi scelestus tantum petit. ad aliam tabernam ibo neque umquam. . . .'

'procax es, Pseudole' interpellat lanius. 'per iocum sine dubio hoc dicis. in hac via nemo carnem meliorem habet, ut bene scis. hoc pretium non est magnum. si autem multum emes, pretium fortasse minuetur. dominus tuus, ut audivi, hodie cenam amicis suis dabit. nonne porcum emes?'

cui Pseudolus 'quem porcum mihi vendere vis? ille est pinguis. da mihi illum!'

'ille porcus heri in meis agris pascebatur, mea manu curabatur. nullum porcum meliorem in hac urbe emes. senatori Romano illum vendere volo. itaque tibi decem denariis eum vendam.'

'decem denariis? immo quinque!'

'octo!'

'octo, si ille lepus quoque addetur gratis. si non, nihil emam et ad aliam tabernam ibo.'

'non sine causa tu vocaris Pseudolus. vos servi, non nos lanii, recte praedones vocamini.'

multum et diu clamat lanius, sed Pseudolus nihil respondet. tandem lanius octo denarios invitus accipit; porcum et leporem Pseudolo tradit. iam Pseudolus noster rediit et totam fabulam nobis narravit. in animo habet leporem amico vendere et pecuniam sibi retinere."

"minime vero!" clamavit Aurelia, quae culinam intraverat et omnia audiverat. "Syre, da mihi leporem! Pseudolus ad villam rusticam mittetur. vos quoque puniemini omnes."

quintus, -a, -um, fifth
culina, -ae (*f*), kitchen
cachinnus, -i (*m*), laughter
iocus, -i (*m*), joke, funny story
videtur, he is seen, seems
lanius, -i (*m*), butcher
caro, carnis (*f*), meat
quanti? how much?
perna, -ae (*f*), ham
pretium, -i (*n*), price
praedo, praedonis (*m*), robber

quidem, indeed
umquam, ever
procax, procacis, insolent, cheeky
autem, however
pinguis, pinguis, pingue, fat
denarius, -i (*m*), denarius (silver coin)
lepus, leporis (*m*), hare
gratis, for nothing
recte, rightly, properly

minuo, minuere (3), **minui, minutum,** to lessen, reduce
pasco, pascere (3), **pavi, pastum,** to feed, pasture
addo, addere (3), **addidi, additum,** to add
accipio, accipere (3), **accepi, acceptum,** to receive

Exercise 30a

Using story 30 as a guide, translate the following sentences into Latin:
1 We were all pleased by the excellent joke.
2 Pseudolus, you seem to be not a slave but a merchant.
3 If I buy a lot, perhaps the price will be reduced.
4 That pig will be fed in my own fields.
5 If that hare is added, I will buy the pig.
6 All the slaves too will be punished.

Exercise 30b

Translate:
in triclinio: Pseudolus, Syrus, alii servi.

SYRUS: eho! domina sine dubio irata est hodie. ad villam mitteris, Pseudole. eheu! nos quoque puniemur omnes.

PSEUDOLUS: ego non commoveor. si ad villam mittar, multos lepores ipse in agris captare potero.

SYRUS: minime vero! in villa enim servi semper custodiuntur neque errare possunt. id nescire videris.

PSEUDOLUS: sine dubio vos puniemini si non statim hos lectos movebitis. ad villam mittar. esto! hic laborare nolo. vos lectos movete! ego fabulam vobis narrabo.

SYRUS: tace, Pseudole! fabulis tuis saepe delectamur, sed si cachinnus audietur, . . .

PSEUDOLUS: nolite timere! domina fortasse me reprehendit sed Cornelius non me ad villam mittet. hic certe retinebor. saepe enim dominus me ad forum mittit ubi aliquid parvo pretio emere vult.

capto (1), to catch   **esto,** so be it

Use of the Ablative Case after Passive Verbs

1 If the action of the verb is carried out by a *person*, "by" is expressed by the preposition **a** or **ab** with the *ablative case*:

e.g. onera a servis portantur.
The loads are carried by the slaves.

2 If a *thing*, not a person, is involved, the ablative case *without a preposition* is used:

e.g. ioco optimo delectamur.
We are amused by a very good joke.

Exercise 30c

Select the appropriate verb and translate:

1 (a) pueros Romanos patres saepe _____.
  (b) pueri Romani a patribus _____.
     (verberant/verberamus/verberantur)

2 (a) uxores Romanae a viris semper _____.
  (b) uxores viri Romani semper _____.
     (amabant/amabantur/amatis)

3 (a) hic liber a me tibi _____ .
  (b) hunc librum tibi _____ .
      (dabitur/dabit/dabo)

4 (a) omnes convivae cibo magnopere _____ .
  (b) omnes convivas cibus magnopere _____ .
      (delectant/delectat/delectantur)

is and ille

		M.	F.	N.	M.	F.	N.
	Nom.	is	ea	id	ille	illa	illud
	Acc.	eum	eam	id	illum	illam	illud
S	Gen.	eius	eius	eius	illius	illius	illius
	Dat.	ei	ei	ei	illi	illi	illi
	Abl.	eo	ea	eo	illo	illa	illo
	Nom.	ei	eae	ea	illi	illae	illa
	Acc.	eos	eas	ea	illos	illas	illa
P	Gen.	eorum	earum	eorum	illorum	illarum	illorum
	Dat.	eis	eis	eis	illis	illis	illis
	Abl.	eis	eis	eis	illis	illis	illis

These words are sometimes used as *pronouns* (he, she, it, him, her, etc.), sometimes as *demonstrative adjectives* (that, those), e.g.

(a) pronouns:
  eam in urbem ducere volo. — *I wish to take **her** to the city.*
  crines **eius** curabant duae ancillae. — *Two maids were doing **her** hair.*
  quis ad **eos** auxilium feret? — *Who will bring help to **them**?*
  glires optimos **ille** vendit. — ***He** sells choice dormice.*

(b) demonstrative adjectives:
  advenerunt ad **eam** tabernam. — *They arrived at **that** shop.*
  vidistine **illam** lecticam? — *Did you see **that** litter?*
  ille lepus addetur gratis. — ***That** hare will be added free.*
  quid **eis** liberis accidet? — *What will happen to **those** children?*

Exercise 30d

in Via Sacra

(A great man in Rome would normally have men of lower rank—**clientes**—who looked upon him as their patron—**patronus**—and attended him on public occasions. Clients who came along unbidden with their master to a **cena** were referred to scornfully as **umbrae**—"shadows". In this conversation, the brothers Vibidius and Servilius discuss how to get Gaius to invite them to his dinner party as members of Messalla's retinue.)

VIBIDIUS: ecce, mi frater! videsne illam domum? est ea de qua tibi saepe dixi. ibi enim multae et optimae cenae dantur. eae cenae sunt per totam urbem celebres. hodie, ut dicunt omnes, dominus eius domus multos convivas ad cenam accipiet. optima cena ab eo dabitur. ab omnibus multum vinum bibetur et multae fabulae narrabuntur. ego et tu invitabimur? mox sciemus. ecce enim appropinquat dominus ipse, Gaius Cornelius, qui a quattuor servis in lectica maxima portatur.

SERVILIUS: at nos ei domino non noti sumus. quomodo ab eo ad cenam invitabimur?

VIBIDIUS: sine dubio is ad Forum portabitur et extra Curiam deponetur. tum in Curiam intrabit solus. eo ipso tempore quo e lectica descendet, nos ei occurremus et dicemus "nonne tu es Gaius Cornelius, amicus nostri patroni Messallae, cuius clientes fidelissimi sumus? numquam sine nobis ad cenam venit Messalla."

SERVILIUS: tum Gaius nos invitabit ad cenam?

VIBIDIUS: fortasse.

SERVILIUS: fortasse? minime vero! nos vocabit umbras, non clientes Messallae.

celeber, celebris, celebre, famous
notus, -a, -um, known
fidelis, -is, -e, faithful

Roman Meals

The most substantial meal of the day was the dinner (**cena**), eaten in the late afternoon, while it was still daylight; the richer classes, who could afford lamps or torches, sometimes began later or prolonged the dinner farther into the evening.

Earlier in the day the Romans ate little; in the early morning they took only a drink of water or wine and a piece of bread; this was called **ientaculum**, and was similar to the "continental" rolls and coffee of the present day. The midday meal (**prandium**) would also be cold, possibly something left over from the previous day's **cena**; this also was merely a snack.

In the early days of Rome, the dinner was eaten in the **atrium**, but as manners became more sophisticated, a special room was set aside as a dining room. From the second century BC, the adoption of the Greek custom of reclining at meals demanded a special arrangement of couches and tables which was known as the **triclinium**. In this arrangement, three couches (**lecti**) were set round a table or several small tables, and the name **triclinium** came to be used for the dining room itself. Men reclined at an angle to the table, leaning on the left elbow and leaving the right hand free. Women, if present, sat.

Slaves cut up the food before serving so that the diners could eat with one hand. Though the Romans had spoons and knives, food was generally conveyed to the mouth by the fingers. Napkins (**mappae**) were sometimes provided by the host; guests often brought their own napkins and carried away with them any food they did not eat from their own portions.

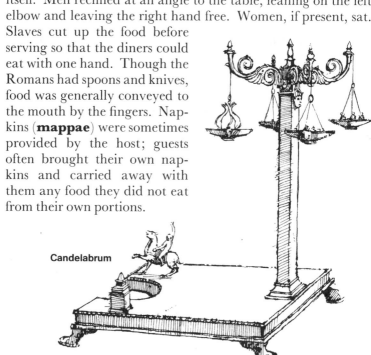

Candelabrum

31
Preparations for Dinner

abhinc tres dies amici quidam a Gaio Cornelio ad cenam invitati
sunt. iam dies cenae aderat. mane Aurelia in foro glires emit.
servi quoque in forum missi sunt. a Pseudolo porcus allatus est,
ab aliis servis holera, panis, pulli. ova quoque et mala et multa
alia comparata sunt, nam cum senator Romanus amicos ad
cenam invitavit, cena optima paratur.

iam hora cenae appropinquabat. dum in culina cibus
coquebatur, ancillae triclinium parabant. mensa a servis in
medium triclinium iam allata erat; tres lecti circum mensam
positi erant.

triclinium Cornelii erat pulcherrimum atque ornatissimum.
in muris erant picturae pulcherrimae. in alia pictura canis
Cerberus e regno Plutonis extrahebatur, in alia Mercurius ad
Charonem mortuos adducebat, in alia Orpheus ad Plutonem
descendebat.

Cornelius servos festinare iubebat, nam iam erat nona hora.
Aurelia, semper sollicita, ancillas vehementer incitabat. mox
adveniebant convivae. mappas secum ferebant quod post
cenam in mappis cibum auferre eis licebat. paulisper in atrio
stabant, Cornelium exspectantes. tandem a Cornelio ipso
comiter salutati sunt.

invitati sunt, (they) were
  invited
allatus est, (it) was brought
  in
holus, holeris (*n*), vegetable
panis, panis (*m*), bread
pullus, -i (*m*), chicken
ovum, -i (*n*), egg
malum, -i (*n*), apple
comparata sunt, (they)
  were bought

mensa, -ae (*f*), table
allata erat, (it) had been
  brought in
circum (+ *acc.*), around
pulcherrimus, -a, -um,
  very beautiful
regnum, -i (*n*), kingdom
nonus, -a, -um, ninth
conviva, -ae (*m*), guest
comiter, courteously, in a
  friendly way

coquo, coquere (3), **coxi, coctum,** to cook

VERBS: Perfect and Pluperfect Indicative Passive

Look at these examples of
(a) **Perfect Indicative Passive:**
amici **invitati sunt.**
Friends **were invited (have been invited).**

porcus **allatus est.**
A pig **was brought (has been brought).**

(b) **Pluperfect Indicative Passive:**
mensa **allata erat.**
The table **had been brought in.**

tres lecti **positi erant.**
Three couches **had been placed.**

It is obvious from these examples that the forms of the *perfect* and *pluperfect indicative passive* are *not* similar to the corresponding forms in the active tenses. The complete tenses are:

Perfect Indicative Passive		Pluperfect Indicative Passive	
portatus sum	portati sumus	portatus eram	portati eramus
portatus es	portati estis	portatus eras	portati eratis
portatus est	portati sunt	portatus erat	portati erant

All verbs follow the same pattern. The following notes explain how they are formed:

1 **portatus** is formed from the supine **portatum** by changing the **-um** to **-us, -a, -um** (like **magnus, -a, -um**). This form is called the *perfect participle passive* and it means literally "having been carried".

2 To this is added **sum, es, est, sumus, estis, sunt** to produce the perfect indicative passive, and **eram, eras, erat, eramus, eratis, erant** to produce the pluperfect indicative passive.

3 The perfect participle passive agrees in gender, number and case with the subject, e.g.

puer laudat**us** est.	*The boy has been (was) praised.*
mater laudat**a** est.	*The mother has been (was) praised.*
aedificium laudat**um** est.	*The building has been (was) praised.*
pueri laudat**i** sunt.	*The boys have been (were) praised.*
matres laudat**ae** sunt.	*The mothers have been (were) praised.*
aedificia laudat**a** sunt.	*The buildings have been (were) praised.*

Exercise 31a

Translate into English:
1 servi ioco delectati sunt.
2 ex culina magnus cachinnus auditus erat.
3 porcus emptus erat.
4 lepus gratis additus est.
5 a lanio octo denarii accepti erant.
6 porcus Pseudolo traditus est.
7 ab Aurelia glires empti erant.
8 ova a servis allata erant.
9 triclinium ab ancillis paratum est.
10 mappae a convivis latae erant.
11 ancillae ab Aurelia incitatae sunt.
12 regnum Plutonis a cane Cerbero custoditum erat.

Exercise 31b

Using story 31 as a guide, translate into Latin:
1 A fat pig was brought by Pseudolus.
2 Three couches had been placed round the table by the slaves.
3 Food has been cooked in the kitchen by the slaves.
4 The slaves had been ordered by Cornelius to hurry.
5 The dog Cerberus was dragged from the kingdom of Pluto.

32
At Dinner

iam advenerant convivae, in quibus erant complures clientes qui ad cenam invitati erant. Cornelius ipse eos in atrio salutavit. aberat nemo nisi Titus Cornelius, patruus Marci. paulisper eum exspectabant omnes; sed tandem, quod ille non advenerat, convivae in triclinium ducti sunt. soleae depositae a servis ablatae sunt. omnes in lectis accubuerunt et cenam exspectabant.

primum aqua ab ancillis portatur et convivae manus lavant. deinde fercula ex culina efferuntur, in quibus est gustatio— olivae nigrae et asparagus. haec ab omnibus eduntur. interea a convivis multae fabulae narrantur, multa de rebus urbanis dicuntur. omnes aliquid novi audire volunt.

tum servi gustationem auferunt; deinde ab eisdem servis magnum ferculum in triclinium fertur, in media mensa ponitur. in eo est porcus ingens et circum porcum glires quos Aurelia emerat. dum convivae haec spectant, extra triclinium magnus

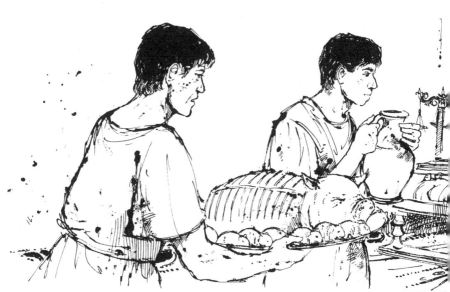

tumultus auditur. subito in triclinium magno cum strepitu irrumpit Titus Cornelius.

mussant convivae "cur Titus noster sero venire solet neque se excusat umquam?"

at Titus, ad locum suum lente ambulans, "salvete, amici omnes!" inquit. "salve, mi frater! amico cuidam in popina occurri."

Gaius, quamquam iratissimus erat, nihil tamen dixit quod hoc tempore fratrem reprehendere nolebat. statim signum servis dedit. tum ex eis alii porcum scindebant, alii carnem ad convivas portabant. non omnibus de porco datum est: clientibus quidem data sunt pullorum frusta.

Gaius servo "puer," inquit "da fratri meo quoque frusta pulli! noli ei de porco dare!"

nunc omnes cibum habebant. omnes cenam laudabant. etiam clientes, quamquam frusta modo habebant, una cum ceteris clamabant "euge! Gaius Cornelius cenam optimam dare solet. nemo meliorem coquum habet. nonne coquum ipsum laudare debemus?"

itaque coquus vocatus ab omnibus laudatus est.

tandem fercula a servis ablata sunt. simul Gaius servos iussit secundas mensas in triclinium portare. servi, quamquam defessi erant, huc illuc currebant. uvae, mala, pira in triclinium portata sunt. vinum quoque in mensa positum omnibus est datum.

inter (+ *acc.*), between, among
complures, -es, -a, several
solea, -ae (*f*), sandal
ferculum, -i (*n*), dish, tray
gustatio, -onis (*f*), hors d'oeuvre, first course
niger, nigra, nigrum, black
res urbanae, affairs of the town
idem, eadem, idem, the same
popina, -ae (*f*), eating-house, bar

iratissimus, -a, -um, very angry
de porco datum est, some pork was given
frustum, -i (*n*), scrap
una, together
ceteri, -ae, -a, the rest
euge! hurray!
coquus, -i (*m*), cook
secundae mensae, second course
uva, -ae (*f*), grape
pirum, -i (*n*), pear

accumbo, accumbere (3), **accubui, accubitum,** to recline
edo, edere (3), **edi, esum,** to eat
scindo, scindere (3), **scidi, scissum,** to carve
debeo, debere (2), **debui, debitum,** to owe, (one) ought

VERBS: Participles I

Perfect Participle Passive
Look at the following sentence:

coquus vocatus ab omnibus laudatus est.

On page 26 you learned that forms like **vocatus** and **laudatus** are perfect participles passive and that **laudatus est** is perfect indicative passive.

The perfect participle passive indicates an action which took place before the action described by the main verb. Therefore, in the sentence above, we know that the cook was first summoned and then praised.

The sentence above may be translated in various ways, e.g.
The cook was summoned and praised by everyone.
After being summoned the cook was praised by everyone.
When the cook had been summoned, he was praised by everyone.
After the cook was summoned, he was praised by everyone.
When summoned, the cook was praised by everyone.

Similarly, the sentence

Aurelia neglegentia earum vexata speculum ademit.

may be translated in a variety of ways, e.g.

Because (Since, As) Aurelia was annoyed by their carelessness, she took away the mirror.

Annoyed by their carelessness, Aurelia took away the mirror.

Exercise 32a

Translate:

1 convivae ad cenam invitati a Cornelio ipso comiter salutati sunt.
2 ancillae festinare iussae aquam ad convivas celeriter portaverunt.
3 convivae in triclinium ducti in lectis accubuerunt.
4 magnum ferculum a servis e culina latum in media mensa positum est.
5 servi a Gaio iussi frusta pulli fratri eius dederunt.
6 porcus a servis scissus ad mensam portatus est.
7 uvae in triclinium portatae omnibus convivis datae sunt.
8 cena optima a Cornelio data ab omnibus laudata est.
9 coquus ab omnibus laudatus laetus erat.
10 Titus in triclinium ductus "salve, mi frater!" inquit.

Exercise 32b

Using story 32 as a guide, translate into Latin:

1 Several guests had been invited to dinner.
2 The guests had been taken into the dining room.
3 A large dish is brought into the dining room.
4 The dish will be placed in the middle of the table.
5 Outside the dining room a great commotion is heard.
6 The pig was being carved and the meat was being carried to the guests.
7 Pieces of chicken were given to Titus.
8 The cook was summoned and praised by all.
9 Grapes had been placed on the table.
10 Wine had been given to all.

Exercise 32c
Orpheus and Eurydice

Translate:

multae fabulae narrantur de Orpheo qui a Musis doctus erat cithara ludere. in pictura Orpheus ad Plutonem descendit. cur? descendit quod uxor eius Eurydice morte abrepta iam sub terra a Plutone tenebatur. dolore oppressus Orpheus constituit Plutoni appropinquare et uxorem ab eo petere.

ianua regni Plutonis a Cerbero, cane feroci qui tria habebat capita, custodiebatur. Orpheus, quod semper esuriebat Cerberus, frusta cibi ad eum coniecit et, dum cibus arripitur a Cerbero, in regnum intravit. per umbras ibat Orpheus; uxorem diu et diligenter quaerebat. tandem Pluto dolore eius commotus "licet tibi" inquit "uxorem tuam reducere, sed hac condicione: Eurydice exibit ad lucem te sequens; tu vetaris eam respicere. si tu respicies, ea retrahetur neque umquam iterum ad vivos remittetur."

mox Eurydice ex umbris ducta est. tum Orpheum sequens ad lucem lente ascendebat. Orpheus, quamquam uxorem videre valde desiderabat, ascendebat neque respexit. iam ad lucem paene adveniebant cum Orpheus amore oppressus est. respexit. Eurydice revocata ad Plutonem retracta est neque ad lucem umquam reddita est.

cithara, -ae (f), lyre
cithara ludere, to play (on) the lyre
ferox, ferocis, fierce
umbra, -ae (f), shade, shadow

condicio, -onis (f), condition, stipulation
vivus, -a, -um, living
desidero (1), to long for, desire

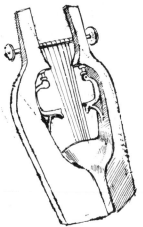

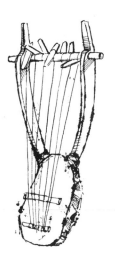

Kitchen utensils

Recipes

1 **stuffed dormice**

Stuff the dormice with minced pork, the minced meat of whole dormice, pounded with pepper, pine-kernels, asafoetida (a kind of garlic), and fish sauce. Sew up, place on tile, put in oven, or cook, stuffed, in a small oven.

2 **salt fish without fish**

Cook liver, grind and add pepper and fish sauce or salt. Add oil. Use hare, kid, lamb or chicken liver; and mould into a fish in a small mould if liked. Sprinkle virgin oil over it.

3 **home-made sweets**

(a) Stone dates, stuff with nuts, pine-kernels or ground pepper. Roll in salt, fry in cooked honey, and serve.

(b) Remove the crust from wheaten loaf, break up in largish morsels. Steep in milk, fry in oil, pour honey over, and serve.

From *The Roman Cookery Book* by Apicius, translated by Barbara Flower and Elisabeth Rosenbaum. Published by Harrap.

Menus

While menus must have varied very much between rich and poor people, and even between the day-to-day fare and the banquet for a special occasion, all Latin references to **cena** suggest that a basic menu was as follows:

1 **gustatio** (hors d'oeuvre): egg dishes, eaten with **mulsum** (wine sweetened with honey).

2 **cena** (the main course or courses): fish, game, poultry, pork, with wine.

3 **secundae mensae** (dessert): usually fruit, with wine.

When guests were present, the **secundae mensae** could develop into a **commissatio** (some form of entertainment), during which much wine was often drunk:

> Look here! You promised to come to dinner and you didn't turn up! It was all ready—a lettuce and three snails each, with two eggs, barley water, sweet wine and snow. Besides, there were olives, beets, gourds, shallots, and a whole host of other things equally delicious. You would have been entertained to a bit of comedy, or a poem, or a piece of music, or all three (I'm so generous!). But you preferred instead the oysters and sea-urchins and Spanish dancers at someone else's house!
>
> Pliny, *Epistles I.15*

> Stella, Nepos, Canius, Cerialis, Flaccus, am I to expect you? My couch, crescent-shaped like a Greek "S", can take seven. There are six of us, so let's have Lupus as well. Among the good things are lettuce and pared leeks, mint, sliced eggs set round lizard fish (served with rue), and a tunny, its paunch dripping with brine. All that will be hors d'oeuvre. The main course will consist of one dish—a kid snatched from the mouth of the wolf that was mauling it,* and meat balls that need no carver's knife, and beans and tender sprouts—workmen's food. Add to these a chicken and a ham that has survived three dinners already; and when you've had your fill of these, I'll give you ripe apples and wine without lees out of a Nomentan flagon. You'll find thrown in, jokes without bitterness and no word you will later regret having said.
>
> Martial, *Epigrams X.48*

* and hence cheaper than one specially killed.

It is clear from these passages that fish of all kinds and vegetables were very popular; and even other dishes were served with fish sauces which enriched, or disguised, the taste of meat or poultry. Indeed, much of a Roman cook's effort and ingenuity was employed in disguising the appearance and taste of dishes.

Clientes were sometimes invited to fill up spare places but they were not given as good food and wine as the more important guests. Here a "client" expresses his indignation at this treatment:

> If you are asked to dinner by the great man, this is his way of paying you in full for all your services. So if after a couple of months he takes it into his head to invite you, his overlooked client (he can't leave that third place on the lowest couch unoccupied!), you're meant to feel your dearest prayer has been answered.
>
> Oh dear me! what a meal! You are given wine that fresh-clipped wool wouldn't soak up. The great man himself drinks a brand bottled in the days when consuls wore their hair long.
>
> The cup your host is holding is studded with beryl. No one trusts you with gold, or if you are given a precious cup, there's a slave watching you, and all the gems on it have been counted.
>
> Even the water is different for clients; and it will be given you by the bony hand of a fellow you'd rather not meet at midnight among the tombstones of the Via Latina.
>
> All the big houses are full of insolent slaves these days. Another one will grumble as he hands you a morsel of bread you can hardly break, or lumps of dough gone mouldy. For your host meanwhile there is kept a tender loaf, snow-white and made from the choicest flour.
>
> You see that huge lobster he's getting now! You'll get a tiny little crab with half an egg around it.
>
> He is served a lamprey. For you—an eel, first cousin to a water-serpent; or maybe a pike that's made its way to Rome up the sewers.
>
> Before the host a huge goose's liver is placed, and a boar piping hot, then truffles. All you can do is sit and watch.
>
> Before the guests will be set some dubious toadstools; before the host a fine mushroom.
>
> Is it the expense he grudges? Not a bit! What he wants is to see you squirm. There's nothing on earth so funny as a disappointed belly!

Juvenal, *Satires I.5 (passim)*

33
The Commissatio

The Roman **cena** was a major occasion in the daily routine. During the meal wine was drunk, usually mixed with water in the drinking-cup (**poculum**) to suit the drinker's taste, for undiluted wine (**merum**) was thick and sweet.

Sometimes the dessert course (**secundae mensae**) was followed by a drinking party (**commissatio**). For this, the guests were usually supplied with garlands (**coronae**) to wear on their heads or round their necks. Originally these were worn not merely for ornament but in the belief that their perfume lessened the effect of the wine. Thus garlands were made with flowers (**flores**), especially roses and violets, and also with herbs such as parsley (**apium**) and with ivy (**hedera**). Later, and especially in winter, garlands were made with other materials such as copper foil or coloured silks. Perfumes (**unguenta**) were also liberally provided at the **commissatio**. These were applied to the hair and face and even mixed with the wine!

At the **commissatio** a "master of the drinking" (**arbiter bibendi**) was appointed to determine the strength of wine to be drunk. He was often selected by throwing dice (**tali**) from a cylindrical box (**fritillus**). The **tali** were oblong, rounded at the two ends, having four sides with the values 1, 3, 4 and 6 respectively. The highest throw was called **Venus**, when the four **tali** used came up all different; and the lowest throw was **canis**—four "ones". Another poor throw was **senio**—a combination containing sixes.

The **arbiter bibendi** decided the number of measures (**cyathi**) of water to be added to the wine in the bowl. He might also determine the number and order of the toasts: the formula for the toast was **bene** followed by the Dative Case, as in a play by Plautus:

> bene mihi, bene vobis, bene amicae meae.
> *Health to me, to you and to my girl friend.*

postquam vinum est allatum, omnibus convivis coronae florum datae sunt. alii coronas rosarum, alii hederae coronas induerunt. Gaius apio modo se coronavit, sed Titus et rosas et unguenta poposcit, nam in popina prope Forum multum vinum iam biberat.

unus ex convivis, cui nomen erat Messalla, clamavit "quis creabitur arbiter bibendi?"

"non tu certe, Messalla" inquit alter. "alii vinum sine aqua bibunt, sed tu aquam sine vino bibis."

cui Messalla "cur non Gaius ipse? quis enim est prudentior quam Gaius? ille enim aquam et vinum prudenter miscebit, neque sinet convivas nimis vini bibere."

"minime!" interpellat Titus magna voce. "hoc modo creare arbitrum non licet. fer talos! non nisi talis recte creatur arbiter bibendi."

paulisper tacebant omnes. tum Gaius "esto! fer talos! necesse est omnia recte facere."

statim igitur tali cum fritillo allati in mensa positi sunt. a Gaio primo iacti sunt tali. "est senio!" ab omnibus clamatum est. deinde unus ex convivis talos misit. "canis!" omnes cum risu clamaverunt. identidem tali missi sunt, sed nemo Venerem iecit.

tandem Titus talos arripit et in fritillo magna cum cura ponit. "meum Herculem" inquit "invoco." tum fritillum vehementer movet. omnes Titum attente spectant. subito mittuntur tali.

"est Venus!" exclamat Titus. "vici! vici! Hercules mihi favet! nunc tempus est bibendi. iubeo duas partes aquae et tres partes vini." primum tamen merum arripit et poculum suum complet. "bene tibi, Gai!" clamat et poculum statim haurit. "bene tibi, Messalla!" iterum poculum haurit. subito collapsus est.

"non bene tibi, Tite!" inquit Gaius. "eheu! nimis vini iam hausisti." servi Titum vino oppressum auferunt.

creo (1), to appoint	**cura, -ae** (*f*), care
prudentior, wiser	**invoco** (1), to invoke, call
prudenter, wisely, sensibly	upon
nimis, too much	**collapsus est,** he collapsed
modus, -i (*m*), way, method	

posco, poscere (3), **poposci,** to demand
bibo, bibere (3), **bibi,** to drink
misceo, miscere (2), **miscui, mixtum,** to mix

sino, sinere (3), **sivi, situm,** to allow
iacio, iacere (3), **ieci, iactum,** to throw
vinco, vincere (3), **vici, victum,** to win, conquer
compleo, complere (2), **complevi, completum,** to fill
haurio, haurire (4), **hausi, haustum,** to drain

Exercise 33a

Translate each of the following sentences in two ways (see page 30) :
1 vinum allatum omnibus datum est.
2 coronae florum convivis datae statim indutae sunt.
3 Titus arbiter bibendi creatus poculum suum complevit.
4 tali allati a Gaio primo iacti sunt.
5 Orpheus amore oppressus respexit.
6 tali a Tito arrepti in fritillo positi sunt.
7 coquus inductus ab omnibus laudatus est.
8 servi a Cornelio vocati Titum auferunt.
9 Titus vino oppressus aufertur.
10 Titus poculum completum hausit.

Exercise 33b

Select the appropriate verb and translate :

1 Cornelius complures clientes ad cenam _____ .

invitatus/invitaverat/invitati erant

2 soleae a servis _____ .

abstulerunt/ablatae sunt/ ablati sunt

3 olivae et asparagus ab omnibus _____ .

edebant/edebat/edebantur

4 quis arbiter bibendi a convivis _____ ?

creavit/creatus est/ creaverunt

5 a Gaio primo tali _____ .

iaciet/iacientur/iacietur

6 a Tito tali in fritillo _____ .

posuerunt/positi sunt/posita sunt

7 Titus poculum statim _____ .

hausit/haustus est/haustum est

8 a servis Titus vino oppressus _____ .

abstulit/abstulerunt/ ablatus est

9 deinde ab uno ex convivis tali _____ .

mittitur/misit/missi sunt

10 coquus ab omnibus convivis _____ .

laudatur/laudat/laudant

ADJECTIVES:
Comparative and Superlative

Look at these sentences:

nemo **meliorem** coquum habet.
*No one has a **better** cook.*

in muris erant **pulcherrimae** picturae.
*On the walls were **very beautiful** pictures.*

cenam **optimam** dare solet.
*He usually gives an **excellent** dinner.*

Adjectives have *positive, comparative* and *superlative* forms.
You can usually recognise the comparative by the ending **-ior** and the superlative by the ending **-issimus, -errimus** or **-illimus,**

e.g. ignavus, *lazy*   ignavior   ignavissimus, -a, -um
pulcher, *beautiful*   pulchrior   pulcherrimus, -a, -um
felix, *lucky*   felicior   felicissimus, -a, -um
facilis, *easy*   facilior   facillimus, -a, -um

These are the forms of the comparative:

		Masculine	Feminine	Neuter
	Nom.	pulchrior	pulchrior	pulchrius
	Acc.	pulchriorem	pulchriorem	pulchrius
S	Gen.	pulchrioris	pulchrioris	pulchrioris
	Dat.	pulchriori	pulchriori	pulchriori
	Abl.	pulchriore	pulchriore	pulchriore
	Nom.	pulchriores	pulchriores	pulchriora
	Acc.	pulchriores	pulchriores	pulchriora
P	Gen.	pulchriorum	pulchriorum	pulchriorum
	Dat.	pulchrioribus	pulchrioribus	pulchrioribus
	Abl.	pulchrioribus	pulchrioribus	pulchrioribus

Some adjectives are irregular in the comparative and superlative:

e.g. bonus, *good*   melior, *better*   optimus, *best*
     malus, *bad*   peior, *worse*   pessimus, *worst*
     magnus, *big*   maior, *bigger*   maximus, *biggest*
     parvus, *small*   minor, *smaller*   minimus, *smallest*
     multus, *much*   plus, *more*   plurimus, *most*
     multi, *many*   plures, *more*   plurimi, *most*

The *comparative* can have several meanings:

     e.g.**ignavior** can mean "lazier", "more lazy", "rather lazy", "too lazy".

The *superlative* also has several meanings:

     e.g.**ignavissimus** can mean "laziest", "most lazy", "very lazy", "exceedingly lazy", etc.

Exercise 33c

Complete the comparison of the following adjectives by filling in the blanks:

Positive	Comparative	Superlative
longus	_____	longissimus
_____	stultior	stultissimus
_____	melior	_____
multus	_____	_____
_____	_____	maximus
_____	ingentior	ingentissimus
_____	peior	_____
_____	pulchrior	pulcherrimus
_____	minor	_____

Exercise 33d

Reflections after Dinner

postquam convivae discesserunt, ne tum quidem cubitum iverunt Cornelius et Aurelia, nam multa de convivio inter se dicebant.

AURELIA: placuit tibi cena, Gai?
CORNELIUS: ita vero! tu quidem omnia optime egisti. coquus nobis cenam paravit optimam quae ab omnibus laudabatur.

quam ingens erat ille porcus! maiorem porcum numquam vidi. glires quoque suaviores numquam edi.

AURELIA: cur tam sero advenit Titus? quid ei acciderat?

CORNELIUS: nihil! amico veteri in popina occurrerat!

AURELIA: in popina? ubi?

CORNELIUS: prope Forum Romanum.

AURELIA: omnes popinae sunt foedae, sed foedissimae sunt popinae
prope Forum sitae.

CORNELIUS: ita vero! iam ebrius erat cum in triclinium irrupit. omnes
convivae erant iratissimi.

AURELIA: fit in dies molestior.

CORNELIUS: sed hac nocte erat molestissimus.

AURELIA: quomodo?

CORNELIUS: missi sunt tali; arbiter bibendi creatus est ille; iussit duos
cyathos aquae et tres cyathos vini!

AURELIA: paulatim igitur fiebat magis ebrius?

CORNELIUS: minime! statim factus est maxime ebrius, nam nil nisi
merum bibit! "bene tibi, Gai!" clamat et "bene tibi,
Messalla!" tum collapsus est vino oppressus.

AURELIA: quid tum accidit?

CORNELIUS: iussi servos eum lectica portare domum quam celerrime.

AURELIA: fortasse cras fiet vir vino abstinentissimus!

CORNELIUS: fortasse!

---

placeo (2) (+ *dat.*), to please
optime, very well, excellently
suavis, -is, -e, sweet,
  delightful
vetus, veteris, old
foedus, -a, -um, filthy,
  disgusting
situs, -a, -um, situated
ebrius, -a, -um, drunk
in dies, every day, day by
  day

paulatim, gradually
magis, more
maxime, very much, very
nil, nothing
quam celerrime, as quickly
  as possible
vino abstinens, abstemious,
  literally "refraining from
  wine"

fio, fieri, factus sum, to become, be made

ab ovo usque ad mala   *from the egg to the apples (i.e. from beginning to
end)*

34
Violence in the Streets

postquam Aurelia cubitum ivit, Cornelius adhuc in atrio manebat sollicitus. Eucleides enim mane ierat ad domum fratris qui in colle Quirinali habitabat. iam media nox erat neque Eucleides domum redierat. quid ei acciderat?

tandem intravit Eucleides, sanguine aspersus. Cornelius "di immortales! quid tibi accidit?" clamavit. Eucleides nihil respondit; ad terram ceciderat. statim servi ad atrium vocati celerrime concurrerunt. Eucleides in lecto positus est et vulnera eius ligata sunt. diu iacebat immobilis. tandem animum recuperavit et lente oculos aperuit. postquam aliquid vini bibit, rem totam explicavit.

"hodie mane, dum in urbem descendo, poetae cuidam occurri cui nomen est Marcus Valerius Martialis. breviore itinere me duxit ad eam insulam in qua habitat frater meus. plurima de praedonibus huius urbis mihi narravit. ego tamen vix ei credidi. sed, ubi insulae iam appropinquabamus, homines quosdam in popinam intrantes conspeximus.

'cave illos!' inquit Martialis. 'illi sunt praedones scelestissimi. nocte per has vias ambulare est maxime periculosum.'

totum diem apud fratrem meum mansi. post cenam optimam domum redire constitui. quamquam nox erat, nihil periculi timebam. securus igitur per Suburam ambulabam cum subito ex popina quadam se praecipitaverunt duo homines qui fustes ferebant. timore affectus, celerius ambulabam. facile tamen me consecuti sunt. ab altero percussus sum, sed baculo me fortissime defendi. tum a tergo ab altero correptus ad terram cecidi. mihi est ademptum baculum, adempta pecunia. abierunt illi ridentes. diu pronus in luto iacebam. tandem surrexi et summa difficultate domum redii."

Cornelius "doleo quod gravissima vulnera accepisti. stultissimus tamen fuisti."

cui Eucleides "ita vero, domine! sed iam prudentior sum. non iterum nocte solus per vias urbis ambulabo."

collis, collis (*m*), hill
sanguis, sanguinis (*m*),
   blood
aspersus, -a, -um,
   spattered, covered
di immortales! good heavens!
vulnus, vulneris (*n*), wound
ligo (1), to bind up
plurimi, -ae, -a, very many
apud (+ *acc.*), at the house of
securus, -a, -um,
   unconcerned
fustis, fustis (*m*), club

affectus, -a, -um, affected,
   overcome
celerius, more quickly
facile, easily
consecuti sunt, they
   overtook
fortissime, very bravely
tergum, -i (*n*), back, rear
pronus, -a, -um, face down
summus, -a, -um, very
   great
gravis, -is, -e, serious
prudens, -entis, wise

credo, credere (3), **credidi, creditum** (+ *dat.*), to trust, believe
percutio, percutere (3), **percussi, percussum,** to strike
corripio, corripere (3), **corripui, correptum,** to seize, grab
adimo, adimere (3), **ademi, ademptum** (+ *dat.*), to take away
  (from)

Exercise 34a

Translate:
1 hic servus est ignavissimus. hominem ignaviorem numquam vidi.
2 Cornelii coquus est optimus. nemo meliorem coquum habet
    quam Cornelius.
3 liberi laetissimi sunt quod cras feriati erunt.
4 ego semper habeo minus pecuniae quam tu.
5 voces pulchriores numquam audivimus.
6 Marcus est maximus liberorum, Cornelia est minima.
7 Gaius domum maiorem et ornatiorem habet quam Titus.
8 ad amicum epistolam longissimam scribam, ad fratrem
    breviorem.
9 Davus est servus optimus. sine dubio nemo est diligentior.
10 coquus plus cibi in culina parabat.

  diligens, diligentis, diligent, painstaking

Exercise 34b

Sentences where a direct comparison is made may take the following
patterns:

  Marcus est ignavior **quam Sextus.**
  Marcus est ignavior **Sexto.**

Both examples mean "Marcus is lazier than Sextus". In the second
example **Sexto** is ablative.

*Using the following lists of names and comparatives make up pairs of sentences on
the same pattern:*
  Names:
  Marcus, Sextus, Aurelia, Cornelius, Cornelia, Flavia, Eucleides,
  Titus, Davus, Pseudolus.

  Comparatives:
  minor, maior, pulchrior, laetior, magis ebrius, scelestior,
  miserior, molestior, stultior, diligentior.

44

ADVERBS: Comparative and Superlative

Adverbs also have comparative and superlative forms.

The comparative ends in **-ius.**
The superlative ends in **-issime, -errime** or **-illime.**

e.g.		
lente, *slowly*	lentius	lentissime
feliciter, *luckily*	felicius	felicissime
diligenter, *carefully*	diligentius	diligentissime
diu, *for a long time*	diutius	diutissime
saepe, *often*	saepius	saepissime
sero, *late*	serius	serissime
celeriter, *quickly*	celerius	celerrime
facile, *easily*	facilius	facillime

Some adverbs are irregular in the comparative and superlative:

bene, *well*	melius, *better*	optime, *best*
male, *badly*	peius, *worse*	pessime, *worst*
magnopere, *greatly*	magis, *more*	maxime, *most*
paulum, *little*	minus, *less*	minime, *least*
multum, *much*	plus, *more*	plurimum, *most*

Exercise 34c

Study the forms of the completed comparison and then fill in the comparison of the other column:

	Adjectives			Adverbs	
longus	longior	longissimus	longe	_____	_____
lentus	_____	_____	lente	lentius	lentissime
pulcher	pulchrior	pulcherrimus	pulchre	_____	_____
fortis	_____	_____	fortiter	fortius	fortissime
brevis	brevior	brevissimus	breviter	_____	_____
facilis	_____	_____	facile	facilius	facillime
tristis	tristior	tristissimus	triste	_____	_____
libens	libentior	libentissimus	libenter	_____	_____
parvus	_____	_____	paulum	minus	minime
ferox	ferocior	ferocissimus	ferociter	_____	_____
audax	audacior	audacissimus	audacter	_____	_____

Exercise 34d

Translate:

1. in villa erant plurimae picturae quarum in una Hercules canem Cerberum vehementissime petit.
2. Britannia ab Italia longissime abest.
3. diutius manere mihi non licet. necesse est mihi celerrime ad urbem redire.
4. hic puer optime scribit.
5. nemo celerius quam frater meus currere potest.
6. Sextus celerius Marco currere potest.
7. de periculis viarum saepissime audivimus.
8. per vias urbis lente ambulare volo.
9. hoc vinum mihi maxime placuit.
10. cras servi mei diligentissime laborabunt.
11. Cornelius iratissimus erat quod frater serius advenit.
12. pueri arbores facilius ascendere possunt quam puellae.
13. Eucleidi praedones pecuniam ademerunt atque quam celerrime discesserunt.
14. Sextus in horto quam diutissime ludebat.
15. pueri quam plurima aedificia in urbe videre volebant.
16. pueri cum servo domum quam brevissimo tempore redierunt.

> **quam** + a superlative adjective or adverb = as ... as possible
> e.g. **quam celerrime,** as quickly as possible

o matre pulchra filia pulchrior	*O daughter more beautiful than your beautiful mother*
exegi monumentum aere perennius.	*I have erected a monument more lasting than bronze.*
fama nihil est celerius.	*nothing is swifter than rumour.*
e pluribus unum	(Why do you think the United States of America adopted this as its motto?)

35
A Letter

Cornelia Flaviae S.D.

hodie Nonis Novembribus illam epistolam accepi quam tu scripsisti Kalendis Novembribus. eam iterum iterumque legi, quod te maxime desidero. quam celeriter tua epistola huc advenit! quinque modo diebus! heri aliam epistolam Brundisii scriptam accepit pater meus. haec epistola a Valerio pridie Idus Octobres scripta Romam post viginti dies advenit!

Valerius, ut scis, est adulescens pulcher et strenuus qui cum patre suo diu in Bithynia moratus est. nunc in Italiam Brundisium regressus est. Brundisio Idibus Novembribus proficiscetur et Romam a.d. iii Kal. Dec. adveniet.

quam libenter eum rursus videbo! sane tamen multo libentius te videbo ubi tu Romam venies! tum te libentissime nos omnes accipiemus!

in epistola tua multa rogabas de periculis urbanis. abhinc tres dies in insula quadam magnum incendium vidimus. nihil miserabilius umquam vidi. quamquam enim maior pars incolarum e periculo effugit, mater et duo liberi quos in tertio tabulato conspeximus effugere non poterant. eheu! hi miseri flammis oppressi sunt. ubi de illa matre et liberis cogito, valde commoveor.

heri vesperi Eucleides noster, ab urbe domum rediens, duos homines ex popina quadam exeuntes vidit. qui homines, ubi Eucleidem conspexerunt, statim secuti sunt. Eucleides effugere conatus est, sed frustra. quo celerius currebat ille, eo celerius currebant homines. facile eum consecuti sunt. o miserrimum Eucleidem! a praedonibus correptus ac fustibus percussus, gravissime vulneratus est. vix quidem se domum traxit.

sed de periculis satis! hodie mater pulcherrimam mihi stolam emit, quae mihi valde placuit. sed tristissima sum quod te non video. fortasse tu Romam cum patre venies. nonne tu patri id persuadebis? te plurimum desidero. scribe, sis, quam saepissime. vale!

-que, and
huc, here, to here
Brundisii, at Brundisium
pridie (+ *acc.*), on the day
  before
viginti, twenty
adulescens, -entis (*m*),
  young man
moratus est, he has stayed
regressus est, he has
  returned
proficiscetur, he will set out
a.d. iii Kal. Dec., 29th
  November

libenter, gladly
rursus, again
sane, certainly, of course
vesperi, in the evening
qui homines, those men
secuti sunt, (they) followed
conatus est, (he) tried
quo celerius . . . eo celerius
  . . . , the faster . . . the
  faster . . .
tristis, -is, -e, sad
sis = si vis

Note that the Romans did not start a letter with "Dear So-and-So".
They put the name of the person sending it (in the nominative case)
followed by the name of the person to whom it was sent (in the dative
case), and after that the letters **S.D.** (**salutem dicit**, sends greetings)
or S.P.D. (**salutem plurimam dicit**, sends fondest greetings). There
was no signature at the end, simply the word **vale**.

Building up Vocabulary

1. The prefix **re-** means "back". Give the meaning of the
following verbs:
  reducere, respicere, revocare, reddere, retrahere.

2. **rapio** means "I snatch". Give the meaning of:
  arripio, abripio, eripio, corripio.

3. Here are some verbs. Nouns derived from them are given
below. Give the meanings of the nouns:

  timeo, *I fear*   **terreo,** *I terrify*
  timor   **terror**

  doleo, *I grieve* **amo,** *I love*
  dolor   **amor**

Now try   **advenio, adventus; conspicio, conspectus;
           descendo, descensus; exeo, exitus; gemo,
           gemitus; iubeo, iussum.**

48

Dates

In each month there were three special days from which Romans calculated all dates:

The Kalends (**Kalendae, -arum** *f.pl*) were always on the 1st of the month.

The Nones (**Nonae, -arum** *f.pl*) usually fell on the 5th of the month.

The Ides (**Idus, Iduum** *f.pl*) usually fell on the 13th of the month.

But in March, May, July and October the Nones were on the 7th and the Ides were on the 15th.

Actual dates were expressed in different ways:

1 The ablative case indicates that the date coincides with one of the special days, e.g.

Kalendis Aprilibus, on 1st April
Nonis Februariis, on 5th February
Idibus Martiis, on 15th March

Compare **eo die**, on that day

2 **pridie** + *accusative* indicates the day before one of the special days, e.g.

pridie Kalendas Maias (lit. "on the day before 1st May"), on 30th April
pridie Idus Octobres, on 14th October

3 A phrase beginning **ante diem** (**a.d.**) is used to express all other dates, e.g.

ante diem iv Kalendas Decembres (lit. "on the fourth day before 1st December), on 28th November.

When calculating, you should include the special day and count backwards, e.g. 1st Dec., 30th Nov., 29th Nov., 28th Nov.

cf. **ante diem viii Idus Martias** (lit. "on the eighth day before the Ides of March"), 8th March.

Exercise 35a

Translate:

1 Kalendis Ianuariis
2 Kalendis Decembribus
3 Kalendis Iuniis
4 Nonis Augustis
5 Nonis Octobribus
6 Idibus Martiis
7 Idibus Maiis
8 Idibus Septembribus
9 pridie Kalendas Februarias
10 pridie Kalendas Iulias
11 pridie Nonas Augustas
12 pridie Idus Ianuarias
13 pridie Idus Novembres
14 ante diem iv Kalendas Iunias
15 ante diem iii Nonas Iulias
16 a.d. vi Kal. Apr.

Now try to work out your own birthday in Latin.

Exercise 35b

Find the exact meaning of the words and phrases in column 1, and deduce the meaning of the Latin words in column 2:

bellicose	bellum, -i (*n*)
emigrate	migro (1)
revive	vivo (3)
hostile	hostis, -is (*m*)
population	populus, -i (*m*)
pacify	pax, pacis (*f*)
Georgius Rex	rex, regis (*m*)
augment	augeo (2)
ultimate	ultimus, -a, -um
Victoria Regina	regina, -ae (*f*)
expulsion	expello (3)

ad Kalendas Graecas   *until the Greek Kalends* (Since there were no Kalends in the Greek calendar this phrase means the event will never happen.)

Roman Education

The Earliest Years—Education in the Home

Little is known about the early training of Roman boys and girls, but certainly the home played the most important part. During the first seven years education was chiefly in the hands of the mother:

> In the good old days, every citizen's son was brought up, not in the chamber of some hired nurse, but in his mother's lap.

Thus we are told Cornelia, the mother of the Gracchi, directed their upbringing. The same was true of Aurelia, the mother of Caesar, and of Atia, the mother of Augustus.

> Tacitus, *Dialogus 28*

The home was always considered the natural place for early training, and the habit of sending children to school away from home, though it increased in later years, was looked upon with suspicion by many:

> Surely it is a matter of great importance that your children should study here rather than anywhere else. Where can they live more happily than in their native town, or be more strictly brought up than under their parents' eye, or be educated at less expense than at home? What an easy matter it would be to hire teachers and add to their salaries the money you now spend on lodgings, travelling and all you have to purchase away from home.

> Pliny, *Epistles IV.13*

This was not the time for formal instruction; it was the home's influence on the child that was the greatest at this stage:

> In ancient times it was the established custom that Romans should learn from their elders not only by watching but also by listening. The father of each one served as his teacher.

> Pliny, *Epistles VIII.14*

The Primary School—ludus litterarius

At the age of seven, if their fathers could afford it, children were sent to school—the **ludus litterarius**—to be taught "their letters" by a schoolmaster, generally called **litterator** or **magister ludi**. The teacher's pay was small, for teaching was not considered very highly as a profession. The curriculum at this stage was limited to three subjects—reading, writing and arithmetic.

Education at home, however, was not unusual, for there was no state education. It was usually in the hands of a tutor, who was either a (Greek) slave or freedman.

Occasionally, we read of fathers who themselves looked after the education of their sons. This was true of Cato and Aemilius Paulus, but note their different ideas and ideals:

> As soon as he began to learn with understanding, his father (Marcus Cato) took him in charge and taught him to read, although he had a very good slave, called Chilo, who was a school-teacher and was already teaching many boys. But Cato did not think it right, as he himself says, that his son should be scolded by a slave or pulled by the ear when slow to learn, nor that such an important thing as education should be left to a slave. He himself therefore taught him reading, law and gymnastics, and also gave him instruction in how to throw a javelin, to fight in armour, to ride and box, to endure both heat and cold, and to swim.

Plutarch, *Cato the Elder 20*

> Aemilius Paulus himself looked after the education of his children. He brought them up in the old-fashioned Roman way as he himself had been brought up, but he was even more enthusiastic about Greek education. For this reason their teachers of grammar, logic and rhetoric, their teachers of sculpture and drawing, those in charge of their dogs and horses, and those who taught them how to hunt, were all Greeks.

Plutarch, *Aemilius Paulus 6*

In schools, discipline was generally very strict. Martial, speaking of one schoolmaster as a "person hated by both girls and boys", continues:

The crested cocks have not yet broken the silence of the night, but you are making a noise by roaring savagely and thrashing your pupils.

Martial, *Epigrams IX.68*

Many Romans followed the Greek custom of sending their children to school accompanied by a slave (**paedagogus**) to look after their conduct, manners and morals.

It is the job of the *paedagogus* to make the boy learn what his teacher has taught him, by encouraging and shouting at him, by fetching out the strap and by using the cane. He makes him do his work by driving every lesson into his head.

Libanius, *Orations 58.8*

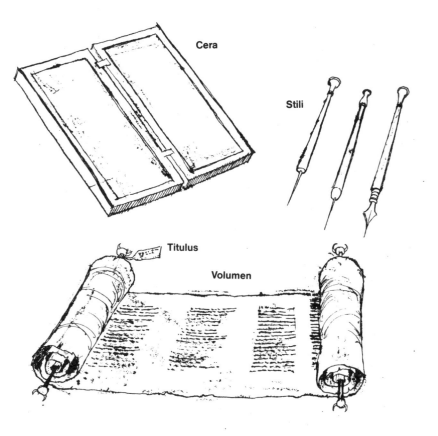

Cera

Stili

Titulus

Volumen

36
Off to School

mane in urbe fuit strepitus maximus; canes latrabant, servi per vias currebant, sed neque Marcus neque Sextus se movit. adhuc in lecto iacebat Sextus et secum cogitabat: "quis est me miserior? cotidie ante lucem mihi necesse est ad ludum proficisci. grammaticum non amo. in ludo numquam laudor; semper castigor. illos versus Vergilii memoria tenere non possum. ille grammaticus cotidie eadem dicit 'tu, Sexte, nihil scis quod semper loqueris' vel 'es puer pessimus' vel 'nisi diligentius laborabis, verberaberis.' itaque domi manere volo."

ita cogitabat Sextus cum Eucleides paedagogus in cubiculum ingressus est. "surgite, pueri!" inquit. "nolite diutius in lecto manere! est enim tempus ad ludum proficisci, ubi Palaemon, grammaticus ille eruditissimus, vos laetus accipiet. vos docebit plurima quae vobis erunt utilissima."

nihil responderunt pueri; inviti ex lecto surrexerunt, vestes induerunt, ientaculum celerrime sumpserunt. nondum lucebat, sed cum Eucleide in vias urbis egressi sunt. lanternam eis praeferebat Eucleides. mox ludo appropinquabant.

cotidie, every day
ludus, -i (*m*), school
proficisci, to set out
grammaticus, -i (*m*),
   teacher
castigo (1), to reprimand
loqueris, you speak
vel, or

paedagogus, -i (*m*), tutor
ingressus est, (he) entered
eruditus, -a, -um, learned,
   scholarly
utilis, -is, -e, useful
ientaculum, -i (*n*), breakfast
egressi sunt, (they) went
   out

Deponent Verbs

Look at these sentences:
   semper **loqueris.**   *You are always speaking.*
   in cubiculum **ingressus est.**   *He entered the bedroom.*

tempus est **proficisci.**			*It is time to set out.*
in vias **egressi sunt.**			*They went out into the streets.*
Brundisio **proficiscetur.**			*He will leave Brundisium.*

You will see that in all these examples the Latin verb in dark type has *passive endings* but the *meaning is active*. Verbs which behave in this way are called *deponent verbs*.

For deponent verbs you need to recognise only *three* Principal Parts:

Present	Infinitive	Perfect	
moror	morari	moratus sum	*to wait*
sequor	sequi	secutus sum	*to follow*

The *present infinitive* of deponent verbs ends in:
-ri for verbs of Groups 1, 2 and 4   e.g. **morari,** to wait
 -i for verbs of Group 3   e.g. **sequi,** to follow

The *imperative* of deponent verbs ends in:

   -re in the singular   e.g. **morare!** wait!
                               sequere! follow!
-mini in the plural   e.g. **moramini!** wait!
                               sequimini! follow!

You have met parts of the following deponent verbs so far:
    moror, morari (1), **moratus sum,** to wait
    conor, conari (1), **conatus sum,** to try
    sequor, sequi (3), **secutus sum,** to follow
    consequor, consequi (3), **consecutus sum,** to
      overtake, catch up on
    egredior, egredi (3), **egressus sum,** to go out, leave
    ingredior, ingredi (3), **ingressus sum,** to go in, enter
    regredior, regredi (3), **regressus sum,** to go back,
      return
    proficiscor, proficisci (3), **profectus sum,** to set out,
      leave
    loquor, loqui (3), **locutus sum,** to speak
    collabor, collabi (3), **collapsus sum,** to collapse

Exercise 36a

Translate:

1 quid puellae facere conantur? puellae stolam facere conantur.
   quid tu facere conaris? ego laborare conor. quid vos facere
   conamini? nos dormire conamur.
2 quando venire conaberis? ego mox venire conabor. amici mei
   quoque venire conabuntur. nos omnes eodem die venire
   conabimur.
3 quis loquitur? ego non loquebar. nos cum magistro loquebamur.
4 quo pueri proficiscuntur? Romam proficiscuntur. nos cum eis
   proficiscemur. nonne vos quoque proficisci vultis?
5 quando pueri e ludo egredientur? pueri e ludo egredientur sexta
   hora. egredietur cum pueris magister? minime vero! magister
   in ludo morabitur.
6 quando tu proficisceris? ego mox proficiscar. puer prima luce
   proficiscetur. servi proficisci non possunt. mox sequentur.

sextus, -a, -um, sixth

Exercise 36b

Translate:

1 paulisper in urbe morati sumus. cur morati estis? ego moratus
   sum quod patrem videre volebam. amici mei morati sunt quod
   aedificia urbis videre volebant.
2 prima luce servi Cornelii in vias egressi sunt. praedones illos
   scelestos sequi conati erant sed eos consequi non poterant.
3 Valerius Brundisio Idibus Novembribus profectus erat sed nondum
   Romam ingressus erat.
4 noli in lecto diutius morari, Sexte. conare illos versus Vergilii
   memoria tenere. fortasse a grammatico hodie laudaberis si non
   nimis loqueris.
5 Cornelius convivis "intrate, amici!" inquit. "ingredimini domum
   meam! vos libentissime excipio." convivae quam celerrime
   ingressi inter se magno cum strepitu in atrio colloquebantur.
6 a magistro laudati sunt quod versus memoria tenere conati erant.
7 tabellarius ab urbe celerrime profectus est quod a principe ipso
   Brundisium missus erat.
8 Cornelia et mater regressae sunt serius quam pueri quod in urbe
   quam diutissime moratae erant.
9 Sextus celerius quam Marcus currere potest sed Marcus iam
   prudentior Sexto fit.

Translating "quam"

You have now met several uses of **quam.** The following clues should help you choose the correct meaning:

1 *In a comparison:*
   clue: **comparative adjective or adverb before quam**—translate "than",
   >   e.g. Marcus est prudent**ior quam** Sextus.
   >   *Marcus is wiser than Sextus.*

2 *In an exclamation:*
   clue: **adjective or adverb after quam**—translate "how", "what a . . .",
   >   e.g. **quam celeriter** tua epistola huc advenit!
   >   *How quickly your letter came here!*
   >
   >   **quam molestus** puer est Sextus!
   >   *What a troublesome boy Sextus is!*

3 *In a phrase:*
   clue: **superlative adjective or adverb after quam**—translate the phrase "as . . . as possible",
   >   e.g. scribe **quam saepissime!**
   >   *Write as often as possible!*

4 *In a relative clause:*
   clue: **feminine singular noun before quam**—translate "whom", "which",
   >   e.g. illam **epistolam** accepi **quam** tu scripsisti Kal. Nov.
   >   *I have received the letter which you wrote on 1st November.*

Exercise 36c

Translate:
1 quam pulcher adulescens est Valerius! libentissime eum
   accipiemus.
2 nihil miserabilius quam illud incendium vidi.
3 mulier illa miserrima quam Cornelia in tertio tabulato stantem
   conspexit ex incendio effugere non poterat.
4 nemo erat magis ebrius quam Titus; ille enim plus vini quam ceteri
   biberat.

5 quam pulchra est illa stola quam mater mihi emit! mihi valde
   placet.
6 milites Romani qui audacissimi erant semper quam fortissime se
   defendebant.
7 quamquam celerius ambulabat Eucleides, praedones eum mox
   consecuti sunt. quam graviter vulnerātus est!
8 quam ingentem porcum Pseudolus emerat! servi ferculum vix
   poterant inferre.

A Schoolboy's Phrase Book

In a Latin-Greek phrase book of the early third century AD,
probably intended for teaching Latin to people whose native
language was Greek, we see an effort being made to overcome
the language barriers created by a multi-racial empire. The
phrases given are designed to help the non-Latin speaker to cope
with the situations he would meet with in a school day.

vado in scholam.	*I go into the school.*
primum saluto magistrum qui me resalutavit.	*First, I greet the master who returned my greeting.*
ave magister.	*Good morning, sir.*
avete condiscipuli. (discipuli)	*Good morning, fellow-pupils.*
locum mihi date. (meum scamnum, sellam)	*Give me my place. (my bench, seat)*
densa te.	*Move up.*
illuc accedite.	*Go over there.*
meus locus est. ego praeoccupavi.	*It is my place. I got it first.*
sedi. sedeo. disco.	*I sat down. I am sitting. I am learning.*
iam teneo lectionem.	*Now I have my reading.*
vobis dico. iam possum reddere.	*I tell you. I can do it now.*
reddo. reddidi.	*I am reading. I have read it.*
muta mihi. scribe. scribo.	*Change it for me. Write it. I am writing.*
nomina accepi et reddidi iterum.	*I have heard the names and repeated them.*

versus postea coepi legere.	*After that I began to read the lines of poetry.*
praeducere nescio.	*I cannot copy this.*
tu mihi praeduc quomodo scis.	*You copy for me as you can.*
deleo.	*I am rubbing out.*
cera dura est. mollis debuit esse.	*The wax is hard. It ought to have been soft.*
scribe tu mihi paginam.	*Write a page for me.*
iam didici quod acceperam.	*Now I have learned what I was given.*
rogavi ut me dimitteret domum ad prandium.	*I asked (the master) to let me go home for lunch.*
et ille me dimisit.	*And he let me go.*
ego illi bene valere dixi. resalutavit me.	*I said good-bye to him and he said it to me.*
postquam pranderam, reversus reddidi.	*After I had had my lunch, I returned and repeated the lesson.*
puer meus, da mihi tabulam.	*My boy, give me your writing-tablet.*
et alii in ordine reddunt ad distinctum.	*Others repeat the lesson in order, according to the punctuation.*
et ego transeo lectionem.	*I go through my reading.*

Latin Phrases used in English

ad infinitum	*to infinity.*
ad nauseam	*to a sickening extent*
ad hoc	*for a special purpose*
in toto	*in total, entirely*
in situ	*in position*
in memoriam	*in memory of*
in absentia	*in absence*
in loco parentis	*in the place of the parent*
in extremis	*on the point of dying, at the last gasp*
gloria in excelsis	*glory in the highest*
in camera	*in secret*
in medias res	*into the midst of things*

37
The Lessons Begin

vix omnes pueri in ludum ingressi erant cum grammaticus ita
coepit: "abhinc tres menses primus liber Aeneidis a vobis lectus
est. quis e vobis de Aenea mihi narrare potest?"

cui unus ex discipulis respondit: "urbs Troia a Graecis decem
annos obsidebatur, sed tandem capta et incensa est. effugit ex
ruinis illius urbis Aeneas, et una cum patre filioque suo et
compluribus amicis ex Asia navigavit, nam terram petebat quae
Hesperia vocata est. postquam multa terra marique passus est,
ad Siciliam vix venit. atque ubi e Sicilia profectus est, maxima
tempestas naves complures delevit. Aeneas ipse, ad Africam
tempestate actus, cum septem modo navibus ad urbem
quandam advenit ubi a regina Didone comiter acceptus ad
convivium invitatus est."

tum grammaticus "res optime narrata est. sed quid in
convivio factum est?"

cui alter discipulus "regina plurima rogabat de urbe Troia, de
rebus Troianis, de periculis itineris. tandem omnes convivae
tacuerunt et Aeneas multa et mira narrare coepit."

hoc responsum grammatico maxime placuit; qui "nunc"
inquit "nos ipsi audiemus ea quae ab Aenea narrata sunt. nunc
legemus aliquos versus ex secundo libro Aeneidis. age, Marce!
mihi recita illos versus!"

Marcus igitur ita recitare coepit:

> "conticuere omnes intentique ora tenebant.
> inde toro pater Aeneas sic orsus ab alto:
> 'infandum, regina, iubes renovare dolorem'."

> *"Silence fell upon them all as they
> broke off their conversations, eager to
> listen. Then from his lofty couch
> Father Aeneas thus began:
> 'Unspeakable, o Queen, is the grief you
> bid me recall'."*

coepit, he began
discipulus, -i (*m*), pupil
annus, -i (*m*), year
navigo (1), to sail
mare, maris (*n*), sea

regina, -ae (*f*), queen
convivium, -i (*n*), feast, banquet
aliqui, -ae, -a, some

obsideo, obsidere (2), **obsedi, obsessum,** to besiege
patior, pati (3), **passus sum,** to suffer, endure
deleo, delere (2), **delevi, deletum,** to destroy

Numbers in Latin

	Cardinal	*Ordinal*
I	**unus, -a, -um,** one	**primus, -a, -um,** first
II	**duo, -ae, -o,** two	**secundus, -a, -um,** second
III	**tres, tres, tria,** three	**tertius, -a, -um,** third
IV	**quattuor,** four	**quartus, -a, -um**
V	**quinque,** five	**quintus, -a, -um**
VI	**sex,** six	**sextus, -a, -um**
VII	**septem,** seven	**septimus, -a, -um**
VIII	**octo,** eight	**octavus, -a, -um**
IX	**novem,** nine	**nonus, -a, -um**
X	**decem,** ten	**decimus, -a, -um**
XI	**undecim,** eleven	**undecimus, -a, -um**
XII	**duodecim,** twelve	**duodecimus, -a, -um**
XX	**viginti,** twenty	**vicesimus, -a, -um**
L	**quinquaginta,** fifty	**quinquagesimus, -a, -um**
C	**centum,** hundred	**centesimus, -a, -um**
D	**quingenti, -ae, -a,** five hundred	**quingentesimus, -a, -um**
M	**mille,** thousand	**millesimus, -a, -um**

N.B. The cardinal numbers from **quattuor** to **centum** do not change their form to indicate case and gender.

The question word **quot?** requires an answer from the *Cardinal* column:
e.g. quot liberos habebat libertus? septem habebat.
How many children had the freedman? He had seven.

The word **quotus?** requires an answer from the *Ordinal* column:
e.g. quota hora est? est nona hora.
What time is it? It is the ninth hour.

Exercise 37a

Translate:

1 pueri novem horas dormiverunt. ignavi sunt. tempus est eos
   excitare.
2 convivae sex horas morabantur. cena Cornelii erat optima.
3 Ulixes multa terra marique passus domum decimo anno pervenit.
4 quot libri Aeneidis sunt? duodecim sunt libri Aeneidis.
5 quota hora est? est sexta hora.
6 quotus mensis anni est Aprilis? Aprilis mensis anni est quartus.
7 olim Martius mensis erat primus anni, et septimus vocatus est
   mensis September, octavus mensis October, nonus mensis
   November, decimus mensis December. nunc mensis Ianuarius
   est primus anni.
8 quot sorores habebat Dido? unam sororem Annam nomine
   habebat Dido.
9 Marcus a grammatico rogatus aliquos versus ex secundo libro
   Aeneidis bene recitavit.
10 Aeneas, ut in sexto Aeneidis libro legimus, in Plutonis regnum
   descendit.

Exercise 37b

Write down in Arabic numerals:
XXX,   XXIV,   XVII,   XIX,   LX,   CV,   DXC,
MDCCLXXVI, XLIV, CLIX.

Exercise 37c

You have already met the verbs listed on the left-hand side. Give the
meanings of the compound verbs:

loquor, I talk	colloquor, alloquor, eloquor
curro, I run	concurro, accurro, occurro, decurro
teneo, I hold	retineo, detineo, contineo, sustineo
duco, I lead	adduco, induco, produco, traduco
eo, I go	ineo, abeo, transeo, redeo
pello, I drive	repello, expello, dispello, depello
venio, I come	advenio, pervenio, invenio, convenio
voco, I call	convoco, revoco, invoco, evoco

Exercise 37d

Kings at Rome Succeeded by Consuls

Romani antiqui regebantur a septem regibus quorum primus erat
Romulus. urbs Roma a Romulo condita est et ab eo multos annos
bene regebatur. Romulus post mortem, ut Romani dicunt, a deis in
caelum ablatus ipse factus est deus. rex secundus, Numa Pompilius,
etiam a deis magnopere amabatur quod ab eo templa aedificata sunt
et res sacrae institutae sunt. tertius regebat Tullus Hostilius, vir ferox,
qui ab hostibus Romanorum maxime timebatur. de ferocitate huius
regis multae fabulae narrantur: a quo Alba Longa, urbs vicina, capta
et deleta est. ab Anco Marcio, rege quarto, urbs Roma aucta est atque
Pons Sublicius in Tiberi factus. tum regnum tenebat vir Etruscus,
Tarquinius Priscus nomine, a quo (ut dicunt) templum Iovis
Capitolini conditum est. postquam Tarquinius Priscus necatus est,
Servius Tullius rex est factus. multa et utilia civibus Romanis ab hoc
rege instituta sunt et pax cum populis vicinis facta est. sed ubi Tullius a
filia sua crudelissime necatus est, Tarquinius Superbus, cuius uxor erat
Tullii filia, regnum occupavit. hic Tarquinius erat septimus
Romanorum rex—et ultimus. ipse enim et nomine et natura superbus
a Romanis expulsus est. tum primum duo consules creati sunt.

caelum, -i (*n*), heaven
res sacrae, religious
    practices

crudelis, -is, -e, cruel
superbus, -a, -um, proud

condo, condere (3), **condidi, conditum,** to found
instituo, instituere (3), **institui, institutum,** to establish

mens sana in corpore sano   *a healthy mind in a healthy body*

The Secondary School– the grammaticus

After five years at a **ludus litterarius** children were sent to a **grammaticus**, a grammarian. Secondary education was more restricted, for only the wealthy could send their children to these schools. Here they studied both Latin and Greek literature. They had to learn to read aloud books in which there was no punctuation or even spaces between words, and to recite them. They also had to be able to answer very detailed questions on every word of the books they had read. A favourite author, from the end of the first century B.C. onwards, was Publius Vergilius Maro, whom we call Virgil. He had written a great poem called the Aeneid (because its hero was Aeneas) about the origins of the Roman race.

Music and gymnastics were regarded as Greek frills not suitable for a Roman.

We can get some idea of what a lesson in the school of a **grammaticus** might have been like from a grammarian called Priscian who lived in the sixth century A.D. Here is part of a series of questions and answers which he gives on the first line of the second book of Virgil's Aeneid:

"conticuere omnes intentique ora tenebant."

"partes orationis quot sunt?"	*"How many parts of speech are there?"*
"sex."	*"Six."*
"quot nomina?"	*"How many nouns?"*
"duo. omnes et ora."	*"Two.* omnes *and* ora."
"quot verba?"	*"How many verbs?"*
"duo. conticuere et tenebant"	*"Two.* conticuere *and* tenebant."
"quid aliud habet?"	*"What else does it have?"*
"participium intenti et coniunctionem -que."	*"A participle* intenti *and a conjunction* -que."
"conticuere—quae pars orationis est?"	*"What part of speech is* conticuere?"
"verbum."	*"A verb."*
"quale?"	*"What tense?"*
"perfectum."	*"The perfect."*
"quomodo dictum?"	*"How is it described?"*
"indicativo coniugationis secundae."	*"Indicative, of the second conjugation."*
"cuius significationis?"	*"What voice is it?"*
"activae."	*"Active."*
"dic passivum."	*"Tell me the passive."*

and so it goes on for many more questions, each word being
treated in the same way.

38
A Lesson for Sextus

postquam Marcus finem recitandi fecit, grammaticus "illi versus bene recitati sunt. nunc dic mihi hoc! quot sunt verba in primo versu?"

"quinque."

"sed quot in secundo versu?"

"octo."

"quid de verbo 'conticuere' mihi dicere potes?"

"conticuere est idem ac conticuerunt. sic verbum saepe scribunt poetae."

"bene respondisti. et tu, Aule, dic mihi hoc! qui sunt 'omnes'?"

"Troiani una cum regina et comitibus."

"ubi sunt hi omnes?"

"in Africa."

"quo in loco?"

"Carthagini."

"unde venit Aeneas?"

"Troia."

"quo itinere Troia navigavit?"

"primum ad Siciliam venit; deinde tempestate Carthaginem actus est."

"multa tamen de hac fabula omittis, nam Aeneas comitesque multos annos errabant antequam ad Siciliam advenerunt. primum ad Thraciam, deinde Delum, tum ad Cretam navigaverunt. cur nusquam moratus est Aeneas, Marce?"

"monitus a dis, Aeneas semper Hesperiam petebat. volebat enim novam condere Troiam."

omnes discipuli grammaticum attente audiebant—praeter Sextum qui dormitabat. quod ubi animadvertit grammaticus, "Sexte," clamavit "expergiscere! dic mihi! ubi est Hesperia?"

"Hesperia? nonne est Graecia?"

"minime, o puer abominande! Hesperia est Italia."

"nil interest" mussavit Sextus.

"at maxime interest" respondit grammaticus, ira maxima commotus. ferulam sumpsit et voce terribili "extende manum, Sexte!" clamavit.

finem recitandi fecit, (he) stopped reciting
idem ac, the same as
sic, in this way
verbum, -i (*n*), word, verb
comes, comitis (*m*), companion
Carthago, Carthaginis (*f*), Carthage

antequam, before
Delos, Deli (*f*), Delos
nusquam, nowhere
moneo (2), to advise, warn
dis, ablative plur. of **deus**
praeter (+ *acc.*), except
quod ubi, when . . . this
interest, it is important
ferula, -ae (*f*), cane

conticesco, conticescere (3), **conticui,** to become silent
animadverto, -ere (3), **-verti, -versum,** to notice
expergiscor, expergisci (3), **experrectus sum,** to awake, rouse oneself

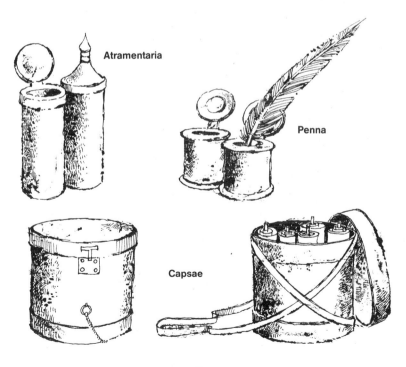

Atramentaria

Penna

Capsae

Place Clues

Look at the following sentences:

ad forum festinant.	*They hurry **to the forum.***
Romam festinavit.	*He hurried **to Rome.***

Cornelius **in atrio** amicos exspectat.	*Cornelius waits for his friends **in the atrium.***
Lucius **Baiis** morabatur.	*Lucius waited **in Baiae.***

ex ludo venit Eucleides.	*Eucleides comes **from the school.***
Brundisio discesserat Lucius.	*Lucius had gone **from Brundisium.***

In the first of each pair of sentences, the preposition and the case of the noun give a clue to the meaning of the phrase. In the second of each pair, there is no preposition. This is normal with the names of towns and small islands.

When the name of the town or small island is in the accusative case, the meaning of the verb will help you decide whether the accusative is the object of the verb or means "to that town", e.g.

Baias laudabat.	*He praised Baiae.*
Baias iter fecit.	*He journeyed to Baiae.*

When the name of the town or small island is in a case other than the accusative, the meaning is likely to be "at" or "in" or "from". The meaning of the verb will help you decide, e.g.

Baiis morabatur.	*He waited in Baiae.*
Baiis profectus est.	*He set out from Baiae.*
Romae manebat.	*He stayed in Rome.*
Roma abiit.	*He went away from Rome.*

domus behaves in a similar way:

domum ivit.	*He went **home.***
domi est.	*He is **at home.***
domo profectus est.	*He set out **from home.***

Exercise 38a

Translate:

1. ubi Graeci belli Troiani finem fecerunt, Ulixes cum comitibus Troia profectus est.
2. domum redire et uxorem suam videre volebat.
3. multis post annis ad insulam Ithacam pervenit.
4. Publius Vergilius Maro Athenis ad Italiam profectus Brundisii mortuus est.
5. Aeneas, qui e Sicilia profectus erat, magna tempestate ad Africam actus est.
6. Carthagini Aeneas breve modo tempus morabatur: novam urbem condere volebat.
7. Hannibal, ubi Saguntum oppidum Hispaniae cepit, iter longum per Galliam et trans Alpes in Italiam fecit.
8. Paulus, dum per Graeciam iter facit, Philippis, Athenis, Corinthi moratus est.
9. mox Quintus Valerius, amicus Corneliorum, e Bithynia Romam regredietur.
10. Roma profectus, Horatius Ariciae in caupona parva pernoctavit; deinde Forum Appii iter fecit.

oppidum, -i (*n*), town
multis post annis, many years afterwards

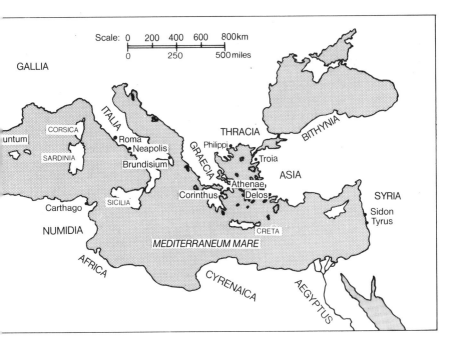

Time Clues

1 *with* a preposition or adverb:

      post multos annos   *after many years*
      ante primam lucem *before dawn*
      abhinc tres dies   *three days ago*
      tribus post diebus   *three days later (afterwards)*
   Clue: the meaning of the preposition ȯr adverb.

2 *without* a preposition or adverb:
  (a) multos annos   *for many years*
       tres horas   *for three hours*
  Clue: accusative case – translate "for".

  (b) tribus mensibus   *in three months*
       eo tempore   *at that time*
       Idibus Martiis   *on the Ides of March*
  Clue: ablative case – translate "at", "in", or "on".

Exercise 38b

The Poet Virgil

Translate:

Publius Vergilius Maro, maximus poetarum Romanorum, natus est Idibus Octobribus prope Mantuam, quod est oppidum Italiae septentrionalis. puer Cremonam missus, ab optimis magistris ibi doctus, sexto decimo anno togam virilem sumpsit. paulisper domi in patris fundo moratus, profectus est adulescens Mediolanum. paucos annos et litteris et linguae Graecae diligentissime studebat. mox, tamen, quod pater post bellum e fundo suo expulsus erat, Vergilius Romam cum patre migravit. dum Romae habitat, versus multis de rebus scripsit et mox praeclarus factus est poeta. in numero amicorum et poetam Horatium et principem Augustum ipsum habebat; sed eheu! saepe aegrotabat et semper infirma erat valetudine. iam quinquaginta annos natus dum in Graecia iter facit, principi occurrit Athenis. qui, ad Italiam rediens, Vergilium secum duxit. Athenis profecti ad Italiam navigaverunt. in terram egressus Brundisium, Vergilius aegerrimus fiebat et in eo oppido mortuus est. corpus Neapolim latum ab amicis tristissimis est sepultum.

natus est, (he) was born	**migro** (1), to move one's
septentrionalis, -is, -e,	home
northern	**aegroto** (1), to be ill
fundus, -i (*m*), farm	**infirma valetudine,** in poor
Mediolanum, -i (*n*), Milan	health
pauci, -ae, -a, few	**aeger, aegra, aegrum,** ill
studeo (2) (+ *dat.*), to study	

sepelio, sepelire (4), **sepelivi, sepultum,** to bury

Higher Education - the rhetor

This was the most advanced stage, beginning after the boy had assumed the **toga virilis** at the age of sixteen. Here he learned the art of public speaking, a necessary qualification for anyone aspiring to high office in law or politics.

A few favoured youths completed their education by a further course in rhetoric and philosophy at Athens or at some other foreign "university".

Attitudes to Education

Horace's father, though a freedman of moderate means, did not consider it too great a sacrifice to give his son the best possible education. Horace recalls his efforts with pride and gratitude:

> My father refused to send me to Flavius' (the local) school where the big sons of the local gentry went, with school-bag and writing-tablets over their left shoulders, bringing their school fees of eight *asses* on the Ides of each month. He dared to take me to Rome.
>
> Horace, *Satires I.6*

Pliny, who showed his interest in a practical way by contributing money to found a school in his native village of Comum, was also concerned that education should be more than book-learning:

> But now the most important thing is who gives him his instruction. Up to the present he has been at home and has had teachers there. At home there is little or no opportunity for going

astray. Now his studies must be carried away from home, and we must find a teacher of Latin rhetoric in whose school we shall find a strict training along with good manners and moral standards.

Pliny, *Epistles III.3*

Petronius also considers that character-training takes place in school and deplores the acceptance of lax standards of discipline:

What's to be done? It's the parents who are to blame for refusing to let their children benefit by severe discipline. But now boys play in school, young men are laughing-stocks in public and, what is worse than either, they refuse to admit in old age the mistakes they learned at school.

Petronius, *Satyricon 3-4*

Quintilian, a famous "professor" of rhetoric in Rome at the period of our story, has a very different attitude from that of the schoolmaster about whom Martial wrote:

The teacher should adopt before all things the attitude of a parent towards his pupils and consider that he is taking the place of those by whom their children have been entrusted to him. He should not have faults himself, nor should he allow his pupils to have any. He should be strict but not harsh, courteous but not lax, lest the former breed hatred, the latter contempt. He should not be bad-tempered, but neither should he pass over what requires correction. When praising the speeches of his pupils, he should be neither grudging nor effusive, for the one will lead to distaste for the work, the other to over-confidence.

Quintilian, *Institutio Oratoria II.4-8*

Finally, two contrasting views:

Who is there who would not recoil in horror and choose to die if he were asked to choose between dying and going back to his school-days?

Augustine, *Confessions I.9*

Thanks to you, I am going back to school and am taking up again the most pleasing part of my life.

Pliny, *Epistles II.18*

39

To Father
from Sextus

Sextus patri suo S.P.D.

ave, mi pater! si tu vales, ego gaudeo. sed nemo est me
miserior. cur me in Italia reliquisti, cum tu in Asiam profectus
es?

primo quidem Baiis habitare me delectabat. ibi ad litus ire, in
mari natare, scaphas spectare solebam. in silvis quoque cum
Marco cotidie ambulabam; inde regressus, cum vilico Davo, qui
me maxime amat, in horto laborabam.

olim, dum prope rivum in silvis ambulamus, Corneliam et
Flaviam magna voce clamantes audivimus. statim accurrimus
et lupum ingentem puellas petentem conspeximus. tum
Marcus, maximo terrore affectus, arborem ascendit neque
desilire ausus est. ego tamen ramo arrepto lupum reppuli et
puellas servavi solus.

at abhinc paucos menses nos omnes, Baiis profecti, maximo
itinere Romam pervenimus. dum autem Romae habito, me
delectat ad Circum Maximum ire. russatis ego faveo qui semper
victoriam habent. nunc tamen miserrimus sum propter
iracundiam Palaemonis magistri nostri. ille enim homo
iracundissimus me, quamquam discere semper cupio, saepe
ferula ferociter verberat. cotidie de Aeneae itineribus multa me
rogat. ei roganti respondere semper conor. ceteros tamen
pueros semper facillima, me semper difficillima rogat. heri
quidem de Hesperia loquebatur, de qua neque ego neque ceteri
pueri quidquam sciunt. immo vero, etiam Aeneas ipse
ignorabat ubi esset Hesperia! grammaticus tamen, cum ego
ignorarem, ira commotus, ferulam rapuit et me crudelissime
verberavit. deinde domum statim ab Eucleide ductus sum.
cum primum domum advenimus, a Cornelio arcessitus sum. ei
rem totam explicare conabar, sed me ne loqui quidem sivit.
iterum igitur poenas dedi.

o pater, regredere, obsecro, quam primum in Italiam! ego
sum miser et valde aegroto. ama me et vale!

ave! avete! greetings!
valeo (2), to be well
primo, at first
litus, litoris (*n*), shore
scapha, -ae (*f*), boat
inde, from there
olim, once, one day
propter (+ *acc*.), on account of
iracundia, -ae (*f*), irritability, bad temper
neque ... neque ... quidquam, neither ... nor ... anything

immo vero, on the contrary, in fact
ignoro (1), not to know
cum, since
cum primum, as soon as
ne ... quidem, not even
poenas dare, to pay the penalty, be punished
obsecro (1), to beseech, beg
quam primum, as soon as possible

desilio, desilire (4), **desilui, desultum,** to leap down
audeo, audere (2), **ausus sum,** to dare
repello, repellere (3), **reppuli, repulsum,** to drive back
disco, discere (3), **didici,** to learn
cupio, cupere (3), **cupivi, cupitum,** to desire, want
arcesso, arcessere (3), **arcessivi, arcessitum,** to summon

VERBS: Participles II

Present Participle

Eucleides, domum **rediens**, duos homines vidit.
While returning *home, Eucleides saw two men.*

abierunt illi **ridentes.**
They went off **laughing.**

lupum puellas **petentem** conspeximus.
We caught sight of a wolf **attacking** *the girls.*

homines quosdam in popinam **intrantes** conspeximus.
We caught sight of some men **entering** *a bar.*

The Latin words in dark print are examples of the *present participle*. This part of the verb has endings similar to those of a

Group 3 adjective, and it is normally translated into English by that part of the verb which ends in **-ing,**

e.g. **intrans, intrantis,** entering
ridens, ridentis, laughing
sequens, sequentis, following

Sometimes a literal translation will not produce satisfactory English. Note how this problem has been overcome in the following two examples:

(a) **ei roganti** respondere semper conor.
I always try to answer **his questions.**

(b) alii **ex adstantibus** aquam portabant.
Some **of the bystanders** *were carrying water.*

ei roganti means literally "to him asking", and **ex adstantibus** means literally "from those standing near". Note that in both cases English prefers to use a noun—"questions" and "bystanders".

Exercise 39

Translate:

1 Aeneas Hesperiam petens Carthaginem advenit.
2 Marcus patrem epistolas in tablino scribentem invenit.
3 adstantes rogavi ubi esset incendium.
4 Eucleides nocte per vias domum rediens a praedonibus percussus est.
5 Davo in horto laboranti molesti erant pueri.
6 mihi roganti puellae nihil responderunt.
7 plurimi natantium scaphas litori appropinquantes viderunt.
8 audita est vox magistri pueros reprehendentis.
9 Cornelius in atrio Eucleidem exspectans ceteros servos in culina colloquentes audivit.
10 Cornelio domo egredienti occurrit Titus, frater eius.
11 clamores gaudentium in viis auditi sunt.
12 Cornelius servis fercula in triclinium portantibus signum dedit.

40
Bored

mane erat. iam pueri ad ludum profecti erant. Cornelia sola in domo sedens lanam sine studio faciebat. iracunda erat quod Baias regredi atque Flaviam amicam suam videre cupiebat. de multis rebus cogitabat tristis, cum mater ingressa est.

"tristis videris, Cornelia. aegrane es?"

"urbs Roma mihi non placet, mater" respondit Cornelia. "totum diem sola domi maneo. mihi non licet foras ire. hic ego laboro sola, sed Marcus et Sextus una cum multis aliis in ludo student. hic nullas amicas habeo. hic ne canem quidem habeo. cur non Baias regredi licet? meam enim Flaviam rursus videre cupio."

"cur Baias regredi vis, Cornelia? Quintus Valerius, adulescens ille optimus, huc paucis diebus veniet. nonne eum videre vis? diu in Bithynia, ut bene scis, afuit sed nunc in Italiam regressus est. nave egressus, paulisper Brundisii est moratus. inde abhinc tres dies discessisse dicitur; paucis diebus huc adveniet. pater tuus diu loquebatur cum illo servo qui epistolam attulit. qui una cum domino suo e Bithynia profectus, e multis itineris periculis vix effugit atque, ut ipse dicit, dominum ex his periculis eripuit."

Cornelia, cum hoc audivisset, maxime gaudebat quod Valerium videre valde cupiebat. "o quantum me delectat talia audire!" inquit. "arcesse, obsecro, mater, illum servum! ipsa cum eo loqui cupio et de his periculis audire."

itaque arcessitus servus rem totam eis narravit.

lana, -ae (*f*), wool	**dicitur,** he is said
studium, -i (*n*), enthusiasm	**quantum,** how much
foras ire, to go out of doors	**talia** (*n.pl*), such things
discessisse, to have departed	

Exercise 40

Translate:

1. Cornelii in caupona pernoctantes mortem timebant.
2. mulieres ad templum progredientes conspeximus.
3. puellae inter se colloquentes multa et mira de pueris narrabant.
4. nos domo egredientes matrem in atrio sedentem vidimus.
5. Sextum arborem ascendentem desilire iussi.
6. a grammatico versus Aeneidis legente saepe delectabar.
7. voces mulierum lacrimantium ab omnibus spectantibus sunt auditae.
8. cum paedagogo libros et lanternam portante ad ludum profectus sum.
9. multi fugientium ad montes ante noctem pervenire conabantur.
10. praedones viro e foro redeunti pecuniam ademerunt.

VERBS: Some New Forms

Look at the following sentences:

> Aeneas ignorabat ubi **esset** Hesperia.
> *Aeneas did not know where Hesperia was.*

> grammaticus, cum ego **ignorarem,** me verberavit.
> *Since I did not know, the teacher beat me.*

> Cornelia, cum hoc **audivisset,** maxime gaudebat.
> *When she heard this, Cornelia was very happy.*

These sentences contain verbs which you have already met but in forms that are unfamiliar to you. Note that the final letters **-m, -s, -t, -mus, -tis, -nt** still show the person endings.

These new forms of the verb will be explained at the beginning of Book 4. In the meantime, you know the meaning and the person; use the English tense which seems to you most natural in the context.

41

A Slave to the Rescue

Quintus Valerius, dominus meus, abhinc duos menses e Bithynia Romam a patre missus est epistolas ferens. ego una cum domino profectus sum. cum quattuor dies navigavissemus, subito maxima tempestas coorta est. navis huc illuc ventis iactata in ingenti erat periculo. tandem cum navis ad insulam quandam ventis acta esset, nos in terram vix evasimus. totam noctem in litore morati, prima luce, quod iam vis tempestatis cecidisse videbatur, in navem regressi sumus.

subito complures scaphas hominum plenas conspeximus. magister navis nostrae, cum has scaphas conspexisset, "pro di immortales!" exclamavit. "hi homines sunt piratae. eheu! effugere non poterimus."

cui dominus meus "si me servabis," inquit "pater meus, qui est vir dives et praeclarus, magnam tibi pecuniam dabit. haec navis est illis scaphis celerior. piratae, etiam si sequentur, nos non capient."

effugere conati sumus, sed frustra. piratae enim, cum nos per mare aufugientes conspexissent, navem nostram adorti sunt. dominus meus statim gladium strinxit et mihi clamans "me sequere!" in scapham desiluit.

ego quidem secutus dominum meum defendere coepi, nam vulnus grave accepisse videbatur. magister navis, cum valde timeret, suos vetuit nos adiuvare. "si piratis resistemus," inquit "nos omnes sine dubio necabimur."

tum piratae, cum nos superavissent, arma nobis ademerunt et nos ad litus adduxerunt. cum primum in terram egressi sumus, piratae circum nos stantes rogabant qui essemus, unde venissemus, quo iter faceremus. omnes tacebant praeter dominum meum. ille enim "si pecuniam vultis," inquit "nullam pecuniam hic invenietis. nos omnes pauperes sumus. at nisi nos abire sinetis, vos omnes poenas certe dabitis. civis sum Romanus."

riserunt piratae, et unus ex eis exclamavit "Romanos non

amo. si vos nullam pecuniam habetis, vos certe necabimus." tum magister navis metu commotus "hic adulescens" inquit "vera non dicit. pater eius est vir divitissimus. ille magnam vobis pecuniam dabit." itaque piratarum alii dominum meum in casam suam traxerunt, alii nos ceteros in navem reduxerunt et ibi custodiebant.

nocte, cum omnes dormirent, ego surrexi, pugione modo armatus. clam in mare desilui, ad litus natavi, casam piratarum summa celeritate petivi. cum casae furtim appropinquavissem, per fenestram vidi dominum meum in lecto iacentem ac duos custodes vinum bibentes. paulisper nihil faciebam. mox tamen alter e custodibus e casa evenit, alter cum domino meo manebat. tum ego silentio ingressus hunc custodem pugione percussi. deinde e casa egressus ad litus dominum portavi, nam ille propter vulnus aegrotabat neque ambulare poterat. ibi scapham inveni quam piratae non custodiebant. ita a litore profecti ex insula evasimus.

iam multos dies in scapha eramus cum a mercatoribus quibusdam inventi sumus. quoniam neque cibum neque aquam habebamus, graviter aegrotabamus. sed mercatores nos curaverunt et Brundisium attulerunt. ibi dominus meus multos dies moratus iam convaluit et paucis diebus aderit.

ventus, -i (*m*), wind	**pauper, pauperis,** poor
iacto (1), to toss about	**verus, -a, -um,** true
cecidisse, to have fallen	**casa, -ae** (*f*), hut
dives, divitis, rich	**pugio, pugionis** (*m*), dagger
accepisse, to have received	**clam,** secretly
supero (1), to overcome	**quoniam,** since

coorior, cooriri (4), **coortus sum,** to rise up, arise
adorior, adoriri (4), **adortus sum,** to attack
resisto, resistere (3), **restiti** (+ *dat.*), to resist
convalesco, convalescere (3), **convalui,** to get well

VERBS: Perfect Infinitive Active

The forms   **discessisse,** to have departed
            cecidisse, to have fallen
            accepisse, to have received

are examples of the *perfect infinitive active.* Two clues will help you
recognise this part of the verb:

    the perfect stem   **accep-**
    and the ending   **-isse**

Exercise 41a

Give the meanings of:
superavisse, terruisse, dedisse, custodivisse, tulisse, coniecisse, fecisse,
conspexisse, mansisse, iussisse.

Exercise 41b

Translate:
1 cum prope rivum ambularemus, Corneliam et Flaviam clamantes
   audivimus.
2 grammaticus Sextum, cum de Hesperia ignoraret, verberavit.
3 Valerius Brundisii paucos dies moratus est.
4 tribus post diebus Valerius Brundisio discessisse dicitur.
5 Valerius vulnus grave accepisse videtur.
6 piratae Valerium rogaverunt quis esset.
7 magister navis, cum piratas timeret, de patre Valerii vera dicere
   constituit.
8 servus, cum in mare desiluisset, ad litus celeriter natavit.
9 Cornelia amicam Flaviam desideravisse dicitur.
10 servus, cum casae appropinquavisset, dominum vidit.
11 cum casam intravisset, custodem pugione percussit.
12 cum neque cibum neque aquam haberent, aegerrimi erant.

Vocabulary

A

a, ab (+ *abl.*)	by, from, away from
abeo, abire, abii, abitum	to go away
abhinc (+ *acc.*)	ago
abominandus, -a, -um	detestable, horrible
abripio, abripere (3), **abripui, abreptum**	to snatch away
abstinens, -entis	refraining
absum, abesse, afui	to be away, be distant from
ac	and
idem ac	the same as
accidit, accidere (3), **accidit**	to happen
accipio, accipere (3), **accepi, acceptum**	to receive, get, welcome
accumbo, accumbere (3), **accubui, accubitum**	to recline (at table)
accurro, accurrere (3), **accurri, accursum**	to run towards, up to
ad (+ *acc.*)	to, towards, at, near
addo, addere (3), **addidi, additum**	to add
adduco, adducere (3), **adduxi, adductum**	to lead on, bring
adhuc	still, as yet
adimo, adimere (3), **ademi, ademptum** (+ *dat.*)	to take away (from)
adiuvo, adiuvare (1), **adiuvi, adiutum**	to help
adorior, adoriri (4), **adortus sum**	to attack
adstantes, adstantium (*m.pl*)	bystanders
adsum, adesse, adfui	to be present, near
adulescens, adulescentis (*m*)	young man, youth
advenio, advenire (4), **adveni, adventum**	to come to, reach, arrive at
aedificium, -i (*n*)	building
aedifico (1)	to build
aeger, aegra, aegrum	ill
aegroto (1)	to be ill
Aeneis, Aeneidis (*f*)	the Aeneid
affectus, -a, -um	affected, moved

affero, afferre, attuli, allatum	to bring, bring to
Africa, -ae (*f*)	Africa (a province in North Africa)
age! agite!	come! come on!
ager, agri (*m*)	field, territory, land
ago, agere (3), **egi, actum**	to do, drive
aliqui, -ae, -a	some
alius, alia, aliud	other, another, different
alii ... alii ...	some ... others ...
alloquor, alloqui (3),	
allocutus sum	to speak to, address
Alpes, Alpium (*f.pl*)	the Alps
alter, altera, alterum	the one, the other, the second
ambulo (1)	to walk
amica, -ae (*f*)	friend
amicus, -i (*m*)	friend
amo (1)	to love, like
amor, amoris (*m*)	love
amphitheatrum, -i (*n*)	amphitheatre
ancilla, -ae (*f*)	maidservant, servant-girl
animadverto, -ere (3),	
-verti, -versum	to notice
animus, -i (*m*)	mind, spirit, will
animum recuperare	to recover one's senses
in animo habere	to intend
annus, -i (*m*)	year
ante (+ *acc.*)	before, in front of
antea	previously, before
antequam	before
aperio, aperire (4), **aperui,**	
apertum	to open
apium, -i (*n*)	parsley
appropinquo (1) (+ *dat.*)	to draw near to, approach
apud (+ *acc.*)	at the house of
aqua, -ae (*f*)	water
arbiter bibendi	master of the drinking
arbor, arboris (*f*)	tree
arcesso, arcessere (3),	
arcessivi, arcessitum	to summon, send for
arma, armorum (*n.pl*)	arms, weapons
armatus, -a, -um	armed
arripio, arripere (3),	
arripui, arreptum	to snatch, seize
ascendo, ascendere (3),	
ascendi, ascensum	to climb
asparagus, -i (*m*)	asparagus
aspersus, -a, -um	spattered, covered
Athenae, -arum (*f.pl*)	Athens
atque	and

atrium, -i (*n*)	atrium, main room
attente	attentively, carefully
audacia, -ae (*f*)	boldness
audacter	boldly
audax, audacis	bold
audeo, audere (2), **ausus sum**	to dare
audio (4)	to hear, listen to
aufero, auferre, abstuli, ablatum	to carry away, take away
aufugio, aufugere (3), **aufugi**	to run away, escape
augeo, augere (2), **auxi, auctum**	to increase
auriga, -ae (*m*)	charioteer
aut	or
aut ... aut ...	either ... or ...
autem	however, but, moreover
auxilium, -i (*n*)	help
ave! avete!	hail! greetings!

B

baculum, -i (*n*)	stick
Baiae, -arum (*f.pl*)	Baiae
bellum, -i (*n*)	war
bene	well
bibo, bibere (3), **bibi**	to drink
bona, -orum (*n.pl*)	goods, possessions
bonus, -a, -um	good
brevis, brevis, breve	short
brevi tempore	in a short time
quam brevissimo tempore	in the shortest possible time
breviter	briefly

C

cachinnus, -i (*m*)	laughter
cado, cadere (3), **cecidi, casum**	to fall
caelum, -i (*n*)	the sky, heaven
canis, canis (*m/f*)	dog
capio, capere (3), **cepi, captum**	to take, capture
capto (1)	to catch
caput, capitis (*n*)	head
caro, carnis (*f*)	meat, flesh
Carthago, Carthaginis (*f*)	Carthage
casa, -ae (*f*)	hut
castigo (1)	to rebuke, chide
caupona, -ae (*f*)	inn
causa, -ae (*f*)	cause, reason
caveo, cavere (2), **cavi, cautum**	to beware
celeber, celebris, celebre	famous
celer, celeris, celere	fast

celeritas, celeritatis (*f*)	speed
summa celeritate	with the utmost speed, at top speed
celeriter	quickly
celo (1)	to hide, conceal
cena, -ae (*f*)	dinner
centesimus, -a, -um	hundredth
centum	hundred
certe	certainly, at least
ceteri, -ae, -a	the rest
cibus, -i (*m*)	food
circum (+ *acc.*)	around
Circus, -i (*m*)	the Circus Maximus
cista, -ae (*f*)	chest, trunk
cithara, -ae (*f*)	lyre
civis, civis (*m*)	citizen
clam	secretly
clamo (1)	to shout
clamor, clamoris (*m*)	shout, shouting
cliens, clientis (*m*)	client, dependant
coepi	I began
cogito (1)	to think
collabor, collabi (3),	
collapsus sum	to collapse
collis, collis (*m*)	hill
colloquor, colloqui (3),	
collocutus sum	to converse, speak together
comes, comitis (*m*)	companion
comiter	in a friendly way, courteously
commissatio, -onis (*f*)	drinking party
commotus, -a, -um	moved, excited
ira commotus	in a rage, becoming angry
metu commotus	frightened
commoveo, commovere (2),	
commovi, commotum	to move
comparo (1)	to buy, obtain, get ready
compleo, complere (2),	
complevi, completum	to fill, complete
complures, -es, -a	several
concurro, concurrere (3),	
-curri, -cursum	to run together, rush up
concurso (1)	to run about, to and fro
condicio, condicionis (*f*)	condition
condo, condere (3), **condidi,**	
conditum	to found, establish
conduco, conducere (3),	
conduxi, conductum	to hire
conicio, conicere (3),	
conieci, coniectum	to throw

conor, conari (1), **conatus sum**	to try
consequor, consequi (3), **consecutus sum**	to catch up, overtake
conspicio, conspicere (3), **conspexi, conspectum**	to catch sight of
constituo, constituere (3), **constitui, constitutum**	to decide
consul, consulis (*m*)	consul
conticesco, -escere (3), **conticui**	to fall silent
contineo, continere (2), **continui, contentum**	to confine, hold
convalesco, -escere (3), **convalui**	to grow stronger, get well
convenio, convenire (4), **conveni, conventum**	to come together, meet, assemble
conviva, -ae (*m*)	guest (at banquet)
convivium, -i (*n*)	feast, banquet
convoco (1)	to call together, invite
coorior, cooriri (4), **coortus sum**	to rise up, arise
coquo, coquere (3), **coxi, coctum**	to cook
coquus, -i (*m*)	cook
Corinthus, -i (*f*)	Corinth
corona, -ae (*f*)	garland, crown
corono (1)	to crown
corripio, corripere (3), **corripui, correptum**	to seize
cotidie	daily, every day
cras	tomorrow
credo, credere (3), **credidi, creditum** (+ *dat.*)	to believe, trust
creo (1)	to appoint
Creta, -ae (*f*)	Crete
crinis, crinis (*m*)	hair
crudelis, -is, -e	cruel
crudeliter	cruelly
cubiculum, -i (*n*)	bedroom
cubitum ire	to go to bed
cui	dative of **qui, quae, quod**
cuius	whose, of whom, of which
culina, -ae (*f*)	kitchen
cum (+ *abl.*)	with
cum	when, since
cum primum	as soon as
cupio, cupere (3), **cupivi, cupitum**	to wish, desire
cur?	why?
cura, -ae (*f*)	care
Curia, -ae (*f*)	Senate House
curo (1)	to look after, care for
curro, currere (3), **cucurri, cursum**	to run

custodio (4)	to guard
custos, custodis (*m*)	guard
cyathus, -i (*m*)	a small ladle, measure (of wine)

D

de (+ *abl.*)	down from, about, concerning
debeo (2)	I owe, (one) ought
decem	ten
December, Decembris, Decembre	December
decimus, -a, -um	tenth
decurro, decurrere (3), **decurri, decursum**	to run down
defendo, defendere (3), **defendi, defensum**	to defend
defessus, -a, -um	weary
deinde	then, next
delecto (1)	to delight
deleo, delere (2), **delevi, deletum**	to destroy
Delos, Deli (*f*)	Delos
denarius, -i (*m*)	denarius (silver coin)
depello, depellere (3), **depuli, depulsum**	to drive on to, drive ashore
depono, deponere (3), **deposui, depositum**	to lay down, put aside
descendo, descendere (3), **descendi, descensum**	to climb down
desidero (1)	to long for
desilio, desilire (4), **desilui, desultum**	to leap down
detineo, detinere (2), **detinui, detentum**	to hold back
deus, dei (*m*)	god
dis	dative and ablative plural of **deus**
di immortales!	good heavens!
dico, dicere (3), **dixi, dictum**	to say
dies, diei (*m*)	day
in dies	every day
difficilis, -is, -e	difficult
difficultas, difficultatis (*f*)	difficulty
difficulter	with difficulty
diligens, diligentis	painstaking, thorough
diligenter	carefully
discedo, discedere (3), **discessi, discessum**	to depart, leave, go away
discipulus, -i (*m*)	pupil
disco, discere (3), **didici**	to learn
dispello, dispellere (3), **dispuli, dispulsum**	to drive apart, scatter

diu	for a long time
quam diutissime	as long as possible
dives, divitis	rich
do, dare (1), **dedi, datum**	to give
doceo, docere (2), **docui, doctum**	to teach
doleo (2)	to grieve
dolor, doloris (*m*)	grief
domina, -ae (*f*)	mistress
dominus, -i (*m*)	master
domus, domus (*f*)	house, home
domi	at home
domo	from home
domum	(to) home
dormio (4)	to sleep
dormito (1)	to fall asleep, be sleepy
dubium, -i (*n*)	doubt
duco, ducere (3), **duxi, ductum**	to lead, take
dum	while
duo, duae, duo	two

E

e, ex (+ *abl.*)	out of, from
ebrius, -a, -um	drunk
ecce!	behold! look!
edo, edere (3), **edi, esum**	to eat
effero, efferre, extuli, elatum	to carry out, bring out
effugio, effugere (3), **effugi**	to escape
ego	I
egredior, egredi (3), **egressus sum**	to go out, leave
eheu!	alas!
eho!	hey there!
eicio, eicere (3), **eieci, eiectum**	to throw out, wash overboard
eius	gen. sing. of **is, ea, id**
elegans, elegantis	tasteful, elegant
eloquor, eloqui (3), **elocutus sum**	to speak out
emitto, emittere (3), **emisi, emissum**	to send out
emo, emere (3), **emi, emptum**	to buy
enim	for
eo, ire, ivi, itum	to go
epistola, -ae (*f*)	letter
equus, -i (*m*)	horse
eripio, eripere (3), **eripui, ereptum**	to snatch from, rescue
erro (1)	to wander
eruditus, -a, -um	learned, scholarly
esto!	so be it!
esurio (4)	to be hungry

et	and
etiam	also, even
euge!	hurray!
evado, evadere (3), **evasi, evasum**	to escape
evoco (1)	to call out
excipio, excipere (3), **excepi, exceptum**	to receive, welcome
excito (1)	to stir up, excite
exclamo (1)	to shout out
excuso (1)	to forgive
se excusare	to apologise
exeo, exire, exii, exitum	to go out
expello, expellere (3), **expuli, expulsum**	to drive out, expel
expergiscor, -gisci (3), **experrectus sum**	to awake, rouse oneself
explico, explicare (1), **explicui, explicitum**	to unfold, explain
exspecto (1)	to wait for, await
exstinguo, exstinguere (3), **exstinxi, exstinctum**	to put out, extinguish
extendo, extendere (3), **extendi, extentum**	to stretch out
extra (+ *acc.*)	outside
extraho, extrahere (3), **extraxi, extractum**	to drag out, draw out

F

fabula, -ae (*f*)	story
facile	easily
facilis, -is, -e	easy
facio, facere (3), **feci, factum**	to make, do
faveo, favere (2), **favi, fautu∘n** (+ *dat.*)	to favour
feliciter	well, happily, luckily
fenestra, -ae (*f*)	window
ferculum, -i (*n*)	tray
feriatus, -a, -um	on holiday
fero, ferre, tuli, latum	to carry, bring
ferocitas, ferocitatis (*f*)	fierceness, ferocity
ferociter	fiercely
ferox, ferocis	fierce
ferula, -ae (*f*)	cane
festino (1)	to hurry
fidelis, -is, -e	faithful
filia, -ae (*f*)	daughter
filius, -i (*m*)	son
finis, finis (*m*)	end

fio, fieri, factus sum	to be made, be done, happen
flamma, -ae (*f*)	flame
flos, floris (*m*)	flower
foedus, -a, -um	foul, filthy, disgusting
foras ire	to go outside
fortasse	perhaps
fortis, -is, -e	brave
fortiter	bravely
forum, -i (*n*)	forum, market place
fragor, fragoris (*m*)	crash
frater, fratris (*m*)	brother
fritillus, -i (*m*)	dice-box
frustra	in vain
frustum, -i (*n*)	scrap
fugio, fugere (3), **fugi**	to flee
fumus, -i (*m*)	smoke
fundus, -i (*m*)	farm
furtim	stealthily
fustis, fustis (*m*)	club, cudgel

G

Gallia, -ae (*f*)	Gaul
gaudeo, gaudere (2), **gavisus sum**	to rejoice
gemo, gemere (3), **gemui, gemitum**	to groan
gero, gerere (3), **gessi, gestum**	to wear, carry on
gladius, -i (*m*)	sword
glis, gliris (*m*)	dormouse
Graecia, -ae (*f*)	Greece
Graecus, -a, -um	Greek
grammaticus, -i (*m*)	teacher
gratis	free, for nothing
gravis, -is, -e	heavy, serious
graviter	seriously
grunnio (4)	to grunt
gustatio, -onis (*f*)	first course

H

habeo (2)	to have, hold
habito (1)	to live, dwell
haurio, haurire (4), **hausi, haustum**	to drain
hedera, -ae (*f*)	ivy
heri	yesterday
Hesperia, -ae (*f*)	Hesperia (the land of the West)
hic, haec, hoc	this
hic (*adverb*)	here
Hispania, -ae (*f*)	Spain
hodie	today
holus, holeris (*n*)	vegetable

homo, hominis (*m*)	man, fellow
homines, hominum (*m.pl*)	people
hora, -ae (*f*)	hour
hortus, -i (*m*)	garden
hostis, hostis (*m*)	enemy
huc	here, hither
huc illuc	here and there, hither and thither
huic	dative of **hic, haec, hoc**
huius	genitive of **hic, haec, hoc**

I

iaceo (2)	to lie
iacio, iacere (3), **ieci, iactum**	to throw
iacto (1)	to toss about, drive to and fro
iam	now, already
ianua, -ae (*f*)	door
ibi	there
idem, eadem, idem	the same
idem ac	the same as
identidem	again and again
Idus, Iduum (*f.pl*)	the Ides
ientaculum, -i (*n*)	breakfast
igitur	therefore
ignavus, -a, -um	lazy
ignoro (1)	to be ignorant, not to know
ille, illa, illud	that; he, she, it
illuc	there, to that place
huc illuc	hither and thither, here and there
immo vero	on the contrary, in fact
immobilis, -is, -e	motionless, not moving
immortalis, -is, -e	immortal
in (+ *abl.*)	in, on
in (+ *acc.*)	into, towards
incendium, -i (*n*)	fire
incendo, incendere (3),	
incendi, incensum	to burn, set on fire
incito (1)	to drive on, rouse
incola, -ae (*m*)	inhabitant, tenant
inde	from there
induco, inducere (3), **induxi,**	
inductum	to lead on, into
induo, induere (3), **indui,**	
indutum	to put on
ineo, inire, inii, initum	to go in
infans, infantis (*m*)	infant, young child
infero, inferre, intuli, illatum	to bring into
infirmus, -a, -um	shaky, frail
ingens, ingentis	huge, big

ingredior, ingredi (3), **ingressus sum**	to enter, go into
inquit	he (she) says, said
instituo, instituere (3), **institui, institutum**	to establish
insula, -ae (*f*)	island, tenement
inter (+ *acc.*)	between
interdiu	during the day
interea	meanwhile
interest	it is important
interpello (1)	to interrupt
intra (+ *acc.*)	inside, within
intro (1)	to enter
invenio, invenire (4), **inveni, inventum**	to find
invito (1)	to invite
invitus, -a, -um	unwilling
invoco (1)	to call upon
iocus, -i (*m*)	joke, funny story
ipse, ipsa, ipsum	-self
ira, -ae (*f*)	anger
ira commotus	in a rage
iracundia, -ae (*f*)	irritability, bad temper
iracundus, -a, -um	irritable, in a bad mood
irascor, irasci (3), **iratus sum**	to be angry
iratus, -a, -um	angry
irrumpo, irrumpere (3), **irrupi, irruptum**	to burst in, attack
is, ea, id	that; he, she, it
ita	thus, in this way
Italia, -ae (*f*)	Italy
itaque	therefore, and so
iter, itineris (*n*)	route, journey, way
iterum	again, a second time
iubeo, iubere (2), **iussi, iussum**	to order

K | **Kalendae, -arum** (*f.pl*) | the Kalends, 1st day in month |

L | | |
|---|---|
| **laboro** (1) | to work |
| **lacrimo** (1) | to weep, cry |
| **laetus, -a, -um** | joyful, happy |
| **lana, -ae** (*f*) | wool |
| **lanius, -i** (*m*) | butcher |
| **lanterna, -ae** (*f*) | lantern |
| **lapis, lapidis** (*m*) | stone |
| **latro** (1) | to bark |

laudo (1)	to praise
lavo, lavare (1), **lavi,**	
lavatum or **lotum**	to wash
lectica, -ae (*f*)	litter
lego, legere (3), **legi, lectum**	to read
lente	slowly
lentus, -a, -um	slow
lepus, leporis (*m*)	hare
libens, libentis	glad
libenter	gladly
liber, libri (*m*)	book
liberi, -orum (*m.pl*)	children
libertus, -i (*m*)	freedman
licet, licere (2), **licuit**	it is allowed
ligo (1)	to bind
lingua, -ae (*f*)	tongue, language
littera, -ae (*f*)	letter (of alphabet)
litterae, -arum (*f.pl*)	letter, epistle
litus, litoris (*n*)	shore
locus, -i (*m*)	place
longe	far
longus, -a, -um	long
loquor, loqui (3), **locutus sum**	to speak
lucet	it is light
ludo, ludere (3), **lusi, lusum**	to play
ludus, -i (*m*)	game, school
lupus, -i (*m*)	wolf
lutum, -i (*n*)	mud
lux, lucis (*f*)	light
prima lux	dawn
M magis	more
magister, magistri (*m*)	schoolmaster
magnopere	greatly
magnus, -a, -um	great, big
maior, maioris	greater
male	badly
malum, -i (*n*)	apple
malus, -a, -um	bad, evil
mane	in the morning, early
maneo, manere (2), **mansi,**	
mansum	to remain
manus, manus (*f*)	hand
mappa, -ae (*f*)	napkin
mare, maris (*n*)	sea
mater, matris (*f*)	mother
maxime	most, very much
maximus, -a, -um	greatest, very great

mecum	with me
Mediolanum, -i (*n*)	Milan
medius, -a, -um	mid-, middle of
melior, melioris	better
memoria, -ae (*f*)	memory
in memoria habere	to remember
mendicus, -i (*m*)	beggar
mensa, -ae (*f*)	table
secundae mensae	dessert
mensis, mensis (*m*)	month
mercator, mercatoris (*m*)	merchant
merum, -i (*n*)	undiluted wine
metus, metus (*m*)	fear
meus, -a, -um	my
migro (1)	to move one's home
miles, militis (*m*)	soldier
mille	a thousand
millesimus, -a, -um	thousandth
minime	least, no
minimus, -a, -um	very small, smallest
minor, minoris	smaller
minuo, minuere (3), **minui, minutum**	to lessen, decrease
minus	less
mirus, -a, -um	wonderful
misceo, miscere (2), **miscui, mixtum**	to mix
miser, misera, miserum	unhappy, wretched
miserabilis, -is, -e	miserable, wretched
mitto, mittere (3), **misi, missum**	to send
modo	only
modus, -i (*m*)	way, method
molestus, -a, -um	troublesome, annoying
moneo (2)	to warn, advise
mons, montis (*m*)	mountain
morior, mori (3), **mortuus sum**	to die
moror, morari (1), **moratus sum**	to delay, remain
mors, mortis (*f*)	death
mortuus, -a, -um	dead
moveo, movere (2), **movi, motum**	to move
mox	soon
mulier, mulieris (*f*)	woman
multus, -a, -um	much
multi, -ae, -a	many
multum	much
murus, -i (*m*)	wall
Musa, -ae (*f*)	Muse (goddess of the arts)
musso (1)	to mutter

N **nam**   for

narro (1)   to tell (a story)

nascor, nasci (3), **natus sum**   to be born

nato (1)   to swim

natura, -ae (*f*)   nature

navigo (1)   to sail

navis, navis (*f*)   ship

-ne   (asks a question)

ne ... quidem   not even

necesse   necessary

neco (1)   to kill

neglegens, neglegentis   careless

neglegenter   carelessly

neglegentia, -ae (*f*)   carelessness

neglego, neglegere (3),
   neglexi, neglectum   to neglect

nemo   no one

neque   and ... not

   neque ... neque ...   neither ... nor ...

   neque quidquam   and nothing

nescio (4)   to be ignorant, not to know

niger, nigra, nigrum   black

nihil   nothing

nil   nothing

nimis   too much

nisi   unless

nocturnus, -a, -um   by night

noli (+ *infinitive*)   do not ...

nolo, nolle, nolui   to be unwilling, refuse

nomen, nominis (*n*)   name

non   not

Nonae, -arum (*f.pl*)   Nones

nondum   not yet

nonne   (asks a question expecting
   answer "yes")

nonus, -a, -um   ninth

nos   we, us

noster, nostra, nostrum   our

notus, -a, -um   known

novem   nine

November, Novembris,
   Novembre   November

novus, -a, -um   new

nox, noctis (*f*)   night

nullus, -a, -um   no, none

numquam   never

nunc   now

nusquam   nowhere

O

obesus, -a, -um	fat
obscuro (1)	to hide
obsecro (1)	to beg, beseech
obsideo, obsidere (2), obsedi, obsessum	to besiege
occupo (1)	to occupy, keep busy
occurro, occurrere (3), occurri, occursum (+ *dat.*)	to meet
octavus, -a, -um	eighth
octo	eight
October, Octobris, Octobre	October
oculus, -i (*m*)	eye
olim	once upon a time, one day
oliva, -ae (*f*)	olive
omitto, omittere (3), omisi, omissum	to leave out, omit
omnis, omnis, omne	all, every
onus, oneris (*n*)	load, burden
oppidum, -i (*n*)	town
oppressus, -a, -um	overwhelmed
opprimo, opprimere (3), oppressi, oppressum	to overwhelm
optime	best, very well
optimus, -a, -um	best, excellent, very good
ornamentum, -i (*n*)	decoration
ornatus, -a, -um	decorated
ovum, -i (*n*)	egg

P

paedagogus, -i (*m*)	tutor
paene	almost
panis, panis (*m*)	bread
parens, parentis (*m*)	parent
paro (1)	to prepare
pars, partis (*f*)	part
parvulus, -a, -um	tiny, small
parvus, -a, -um	small
pasco, pascere (3), pavi, pastum	to feed, pasture
pater, patris (*m*)	father
patior, pati (3), passus sum	to suffer, endure
patruus, -i (*m*)	uncle
pauci, -ae, -a	few
paulatim	gradually, little by little
paulisper	for a short time
paulum	a little, little
pauper, pauperis	poor
pax, pacis (*f*)	peace
pecto, pectere (3), pexi, pexum	to comb
pecunia, -ae (*f*)	money

peior, peioris	worse
pello, pellere (3), **pepuli, pulsum**	to drive
per (+ *acc.*)	through, along, over
percutio, percutere (3), **percussi, percussum**	to strike
periculosus, -a, -um	dangerous
periculum, -i (*n*)	danger
perna, -ae (*f*)	ham
pernocto (1)	to spend the night
persuadeo, persuadere (2), **-suasi, -suasum** (+ *dat.*)	to persuade
perterritus, -a, -um	terrified
pervenio, pervenire (4), **-veni, -ventum** (**ad** + *acc.*)	to reach, arrive (at)
pessimus, -a, -um	worst
peto, petere (3), **petivi, petitum**	to seek, make for, attack
Philippi, -orum (*m.pl*)	Philippi
pictura, -ae (*f*)	picture
pinguis, -is, -e	fat, rich
pirata, -ae (*m*)	pirate
pirum, -i (*n*)	pear
placeo (2) (+ *dat.*)	to please
plenus, -a, -um	full
plurimus, -a, -um	very much, most
quam plurimum	as much as possible
plus	more
Pluto, Plutonis (*m*)	Pluto, God of the Underworld
poculum, -i (*n*)	cup
poena, -ae (*f*)	punishment, penalty
poenas dare	to be punished
poeta, -ae (*m*)	poet
pono, ponere (3), **posui, positum**	to place, put
pons, pontis (*m*)	bridge
popina, -ae (*f*)	eating-house, bar
populus, -i (*m*)	people
porcus, -i (*m*)	pig
porta, -ae (*f*)	gate
porto (1)	to carry
posco, poscere (3), **poposci**	to ask for, demand
possum, posse, potui	to be able
post (+ *acc.*)	after
postquam	after
(se) praecipitare	to hurl (oneself)
praeclarus, -a, -um	famous
praedo, praedonis (*m*)	robber
praefero, praeferre, praetuli, praelatum	to carry in front

praeter (+ *acc.*)	except
praetereo, praeterire,	
praeterii, praeteritum	to go past
pretium, -i (*n*)	price
pridie (+ *acc.*)	on the day before
primo	at first
primum	first
quam primum	as soon as possible
primus, -a, -um	first
prima lux	dawn
princeps, principis (*m*)	emperor, leader
procax, procacis	cheeky, insolent
procul	far
produco, producere (3),	
produxi, productum	to bring forward
proficiscor, proficisci (3),	
profectus sum	to set out
progredior, progredi (3),	
progressus sum	to go forward, advance
pronus, -a, -um	face down
prope (+ *acc.*)	near
propter (+ *acc.*)	on account of
prudens, prudentis	wise
prudenter	wisely
puella, -ae (*f*)	girl
puer, pueri (*m*)	boy
pugio, pugionis (*m*)	dagger
pulcher, pulchra, pulchrum	beautiful, handsome
pulchre	finely, excellently
pullus, -i (*m*)	chicken
punio (4)	to punish

Q

quaero, quaerere (3),	
quaesivi, quaesitum	to ask, look for
qualis?	what kind of? what sort of?
quam!	how!
quam	than
quam celerrime	as quickly as possible
quam plurimum	as much as possible
quamquam	although
quando?	when?
quantus, -a, -um?	how big? how much?
quanti?	how much (in price)?
quartus, -a, -um	fourth
quattuor	four
-que	and
qui, quae, quod	who, which
quidam, quaedam, quoddam	a, a certain, (*pl.*) some

quidem	indeed
ne ... quidem	not even
quingentesimus, -a, -um	five-hundredth
quingenti, -ae, -a	five hundred
quinque	five
quintus, -a, -um	fifth
Quirinalis, -is, -e	Quirinal (hill)
quis? quid?	who? which? what?
quo?	where ... to?
quo ... eo ...	the (more) ... the (more) ...
quod	because
quomodo?	how?
quoniam	since
quoque	also
quot?	how many?
quotus, -a, -um?	which (in numerical order)?
quota hora est?	what time is it?
ramus, -i (*m*)	branch
rapio, rapere (3), **rapui, raptum**	to snatch, seize
recito (1)	to read aloud, recite
recte	rightly, properly
recumbo, recumbere (3), **recubui**	to lie down
reddo, reddere (3), **reddidi, redditum**	to give back, return
redeo, redire, redii, reditum	to go back, return
reduco, reducere (3), **reduxi, reductum**	to lead back, take back
regina, -ae (*f*)	queen
regno (1)	to reign
regnum, -i (*n*)	kingdom
rego, regere (3), **rexi, rectum**	to rule
regredior, regredi (3), **regressus sum**	to go back, return
relinquo, relinquere (3), **reliqui, relictum**	to leave
remitto, remittere (3), **-misi, -missum**	to send back
removeo, removere (2), **removi, remotum**	to move back, remove
repello, repellere (3), **reppuli, repulsum**	to drive back, beat back
reprehendo, -ere (3), **reprehendi, reprehensum**	to scold
res, rei (*f*)	thing, matter, affair, situation
res urbanae	affairs of the town
res sacrae	sacred symbols, sacred rites
resisto, resistere (3), **restiti** (+ *dat.*)	to resist

respicio, respicere (3), **respexi, respectum**	to look back, look round at
respondeo, respondere (2), **respondi, responsum**	to answer, reply
responsum, -i (*n*)	reply
retineo, retinere (2), **retinui, retentum**	to hold back
retraho, retrahere (3), **retraxi, retractum**	to drag back
revoco (1)	to call back, recall
rex, regis (*m*)	king
rideo, ridere (2), **risi, risum**	to laugh, laugh at
risus, risus (*m*)	laughter, laugh, smile
rivus, -i (*m*)	stream
rixa, -ae (*f*)	quarrel
rogo (1)	to ask
Roma, -ae (*f*)	Rome
Romanus, -a, -um	Roman
rosa, -ae (*f*)	rose
ruina, -ae (*f*)	ruin, collapse
rursus	again
russatus, -a, -um	red

S

saepe	often
quam saepissime	as often as possible
Saguntum, -i (*n*)	Saguntum
saluto (1)	to greet, welcome
salve! salvete!	good day! greetings! welcome!
sane	certainly, of course
sanguis, sanguinis (*m*)	blood
satis	enough
scapha, -ae (*f*)	boat
scelestus, -a, -um	wicked
scindo, scindere (3), **scidi, scissum**	to cut, split
scio (4)	to know
scribo, scribere (3), **scripsi, scriptum**	to write
se	himself, herself, itself, themselve
secundus, -a, -um	second
secundae mensae	second course, dessert
securus, -a, -um	carefree, unconcerned
sed	but
sedeo, sedere (2), **sedi, sessum**	to sit
sella, -ae (*f*)	seat, chair
semper	always
senator, senatoris (*m*)	senator
senio, senionis (*m*)	the six (in dicing)

sepelio, sepelire (4), **sepelivi, sepultum**	to bury
septem	seven
septentrionalis, -is, -e	northern
septimus, -a, -um	seventh
sequens, sequentis	following
sequor, sequi (3), **secutus sum**	to follow
sero	late
servo (1)	to save, keep, protect
servus, -i (*m*)	slave
sex	six
sextus, -a, -um	sixth
sextus decimus	sixteenth
si	if
sibi	to himself, herself, itself, themselves; for himself, etc.
sic	thus, in this way
Sicilia, -ae (*f*)	Sicily
signum, -i (*n*)	signal, sign
silentium, -i (*n*)	silence
silva, -ae (*f*)	wood
simul	at the same time
sine (+ *abl.*)	without
sine dubio	without doubt
sino, sinere (3), **sivi, situm**	to allow
sis	= **si vis** (please)
situs, -a, -um	placed, situated
soleae, -arum (*f.pl*)	sandals
soleo, solere (2), **solitus sum**	to be accustomed
sollicitus, -a, -um	worried, anxious
solus, -a, -um	alone
sordidus, -a, -um	dirty
soror, sororis (*f*)	sister
spectaculum, -i (*n*)	sight, spectacle
spectator, spectatoris (*m*)	spectator, onlooker
specto (1)	to watch
speculum, -i (*n*)	mirror
statim	immediately
sto, stare (1), **steti, statum**	to stand
stola, -ae (*f*)	dress
strenuus, -a, -um	energetic
strepitus, -us (*m*)	noise, din, clattering
stringo, stringere (3), **strinxi, strictum**	to draw (a sword)
studeo (2) (+ *dat.*)	to study
studium, -i (*n*)	study
stultus, -a, -um	stupid, foolish
suavis, -is, -e	sweet, delightful

sub (+ *abl.*)	under
subito	suddenly
summus, -a, -um	the top of . . . , the greatest
summa celeritate	with the greatest speed, at top speed
sumo, sumere (3), **sumpsi, sumptum**	to take, pick up
superbus, -a, -um	proud, arrogant
supero (1)	to overcome
surgo, surgere (3), **surrexi, surrectum**	to rise, get up
sustineo, sustinere (2), **sustinui, sustentum**	to hold up, support, sustain
suus, -a, -um	his, her, its, their
T **taberna, -ae** (*f*)	shop, inn
tablinum, -i (*n*)	study (room)
tabulatum, -i (*n*)	storey
taceo (2)	to be silent
tali, -orum (*m.pl*)	dice
talis, -is, -e	such, of such a kind
talia (*n.pl*)	such things
tam	so
tamen	however
tandem	at length, at last
tantus, -a, -um	so great
temerarius, -a, -um	rash, reckless, bold
tempestas, tempestatis (*f*)	storm
templum, -i (*n*)	temple
tempus, temporis (*n*)	time
teneo, tenere (2), **tenui, tentum**	to hold
tergum, -i (*n*)	back
terra, -ae (*f*)	earth
terreo (2)	to terrify
terribilis, -is, -e	frightening
terror, terroris (*m*)	terror
tertius, -a, -um	third
Thracia, -ae (*f*)	Thrace
Tiberis, Tiberis (*m*)	River Tiber
timeo (2)	to fear
timide	fearfully, timidly
timidus, -a, -um	fearful, timid
timor, timoris (*m*)	fear
toga, -ae (*f*)	toga
toga virilis	toga worn by adult male (plain white)
totus, -a, -um	whole of
trado, tradere (3), **tradidi, traditum**	to hand over

traduco, traducere (3), **traduxi, traductum**	to lead across
traho, trahere (3), **traxi, tractum**	to drag
trans (+ *acc.*)	across
transeo, transire, transii, transitum	to cross
tremo, tremere (3), **tremui**	to tremble
tres, tres, tria	three
triclinium, -i (*n*)	dining room
triste	sadly
tristis, -is, -e	sad
Troia, -ae (*f*)	Troy
Troianus, -a, -um	Trojan
tu	you (*sing.*)
tum	then, at that moment
tumultus, -us (*m*)	uproar, din, confusion
tuus, -a, -um	your

U

ubi?	where?
ubi	when
ultimus, -a, -um	last
umbra, -ae (*f*)	shadow
umquam	ever
una	together
unde?	where . . . from?
undique	from all sides
unguentum, -i (*n*)	ointment, perfume
unus, -a, -um	one
urbanus, -a, -um	of the city
res urbanae	city affairs
urbs, urbis (*f*)	city
ut	as
utilis, -is, -e	useful
uva, -ae (*f*)	bunch of grapes
uxor, uxoris (*f*)	wife

V

valde	very, very much
vale! valete!	goodbye
valeo (2)	to be strong, to be well
valetudo, valetudinis (*f*)	health (good or bad)
vehementer	violently, furiously
vehiculum, -i (*n*)	vehicle
vel	or
vel . . . vel . . .	either . . . or . . .
velle	to wish
vendo, vendere (3), **vendidi, venditum**	to sell

venio, venire (4), **veni, ventum**	to come
ventus, -i (*m*)	wind
Venus, Veneris (*f*)	Venus, the highest throw of the dice
verbero (1)	to beat
verbum, -i (*n*)	word
Vergilius, -i (*m*)	Virgil
vero	truly
ita vero!	yes
versus, -us (*m*)	line (of poetry)
verus, -a, -um	true
vesper, vesperis (*m*)	evening
vesperi	in the evening
vestis, vestis (*f*)	clothing, garment
veto, vetare (1), **vetui, vetitum**	to forbid, tell not to
vetus, veteris	old
vexatus, -a, -um	annoyed
vexo (1)	to annoy
via, -ae (*f*)	road, street
vicesimus, -a, -um	twentieth
vicinus, -a, -um	neighbouring
victoria, -ae (*f*)	victory
video, videre (2), **vidi, visum**	to see
videor, videri (2), **visus sum**	to seem, to be seen
viginti	twenty
vilicus, -i (*m*)	foreman, overseer
vinco, vincere (3), **vici, victum**	to conquer, overcome
vinum, -i (*n*)	wine
vir, viri (*m*)	man
vis, vim (*acc.*), **vi** (*abl.*) (*f*)	force
vis fumi	a cloud of smoke
vito (1)	to avoid
vix	scarcely
voco (1)	to call, invite
volo, velle, volui	to wish
vos	you (*pl*)
vox, vocis (*f*)	voice
vulnero (1)	to wound
vulnus, vulneris (*n*)	wound